TRUST MY LOVE

BHAVNA SJ CHUDASAMA

Published by Bhavna SJ Chudasama

ISBN 978-1-8381290-0-2

First published in 2020

Designed by Hawk Editorial Ltd, Hull

For my darling Ma, Susi Chudasama, who supports me whatever I do, and the best dad ever, Jayantilal Chudasama, who tells me I can do anything.

Many thanks to Heena who guided me through the flaws in my characters, Reena and Neha for never reading this book but encouraging me, the overqualified Chandni and sarcastic Amar. Roma for being Roma. To Kristin Taylor, thank you, thank you, thank you, for believing in me and being my guiding light in this journey of self-publishing; without you I would have floundered.

Last but not least, for all those in my life who have been kind to me and had more faith in me than I had – each of you made a difference.

Bad men need nothing more to compass their ends, than that good men should look on and do nothing

John Stuart Mill

CHAPTER ONE

Chrissy threw a pillow at the door, muttering in frustration at the noise Anne was making. Truth be told it was the sound of a famous crooner but at two in the morning, it was enough to grate on anyone's nerves. Why Anne felt it necessary to suddenly pay her and her four-year-old son Nico a visit after a year's absence she couldn't fathom. Anne always knew how to have a good time, but she also knew the walls of the flat were paper-thin and sound passed through them regardless, and she wouldn't let their discomfort get in the way of her plans.

The floorboards were creaky and the roughly laid carpet would somehow manage to rise with gusts of wind allowed to invade this small flat through the old rickety windows and under its ancient doors. Large cracks were forming on all the walls; they were not visible in the dark but starkly noticeable in the daytime. The flat was a bit of a hazard, but their landlord Will had allowed them to live there in addition to Chrissy's wages as manager in the cafe below. It could probably run itself, but Will insisted he needed a manager. He turned out to be a guardian angel for Chrissy and Nico, and had been the reason why their lives were stable. They could hardly make more demands as he was being generous enough already.

Will had come for a visit recently and had been horrified at the disrepair in the flat. He had immediately had a surveyor attend and they were awaiting a work start date any day now, which would entail the cafe closing for two months. Customers were aware that temporary closure was imminent. The surveyor had assured them that it was safe to reside in the flat until the works commenced.

Anne always had her room at the flat although she was hardly ever there. Chrissy wanted her to know she always had a home. It was more surprising, then, that Anne had stayed here for the past three Fridays. Chrissy shared a room with her precious nephew, Anne's son with Nicholas Waite, Chrissy's former employer. It was a small box room on the first-floor flat atop the cafe her parents used to own. Will had purchased it from Chrissy's parents' estate to ease the burden of the future that a 20-year-old Anne and 16-year-old Chrissy faced after they had died. Anne had lived with Chrissy and her family before Chrissy had been born. Anne was her maternal aunt Gemma's daughter, hence Chrissy's cousin, but had always been treated like her sister. Aunt Gemma was a free spirit who travelled the world, but Chrissy was unaware if she kept in touch with Anne.

The flat had two exit doors at either end of a corridor; one led to a set of stairs to the cafe and the other to outdoor stairs that exited the flat directly on to a quiet back road. The two bedrooms, a lounge, kitchen and bathroom led off the corridor. It was decorated with a primrose wallpaper that was peeling off the walls and a dark maroon carpet that had seen better days. It was a small flat but it was enough for the three of them. In fact, only Nico and Chrissy lived there permanently. Nico's toys were stuffed into a big trunk under their box room window; it gaped open, exposing a plethora of love-worn toys and books. Since Anne had come to stay, any sign of a child in this flat was banished to their little box room, which in turn was bereft of any sign of the adult who also occupied it.

As Anne entertained her date in this shambolic flat, Chrissy and Nico huddled together in the warm cocoon of their double quilt. A little lamp at their bedside shone its glow into the small dark room and on to their two bodies. With an extra blanket on their quilt and Nico's cute little form radiating heat, Chrissy thought she could conquer the world as long as he was in it with her. She wondered how the harshness of life after her parents died had seemed like a distant memory once Nico had been born.

When their parents died, Anne and Chrissy had been young. Anne had just started modelling assignments and Chrissy was still at school. On that fateful day, Chrissy had been going to her parents' cafe on her way home from school, to be met with the cafe being cordoned off by police tape and two police cars parked outside. She had immediately panicked and thought the worst; something had happened to her father – and she was right. She was not allowed to go beyond the cordon and Will, a family friend, had been passing by and came to her aid. He comforted Chrissy and told her later that a suspect had tried to rob the local bank, fled without any loot, and had been cornered in the cafe. Her mother Kim had been in the cafe waiting for Chrissy to come home from school, as she often did, when the robber had burst in and grabbed her, holding a knife to her throat. Jay, her father, had run towards them to free Kim, when the robber plunged the knife into Jay's chest. Jay died instantly as a major artery had been punctured.

Though Kim was not hurt, she survived Jay by just six months; her health gradually deteriorated and it seemed that she just did not want to live without Jay. Even the presence of Chrissy and Anne was not enough to keep her with them. Clinically the doctors said she died of a stroke but Chrissy knew she just couldn't live without their father. They had been happily married for twenty-five years but were still relatively young. When Jay had died, Kim and Chrissy tried to keep the cafe running, but they couldn't manage as Chrissy would go to school and Kim would just sit in the cafe not able to comprehend how to continue living without her Jay. The cafe closed within two months of Jay's death. Once Kim had gone, real decisions had to made about Anne and Chrissy's future.

Will saw potential in the cafe as a going concern and purchased the business along with the two flats above. The family home had to be sold, but it had negative equity as Jay had mortgaged the house to renovate the cafe after the area had suffered numerous floods, for which the insurance money did not cover all the repairs. When everything was settled, Anne and Chrissy were left with a small sum that was not enough for a deposit on a flat. Whatever money Anne made would nearly all be spent on herself, and the nest-egg was fast being depleted. Chrissy had tried to do well in school but could not concentrate after her mother and father had gone, so she had left school having only just passed basic qualifications.

Chrissy knew the running of the cafe, so Will had installed her as a waitress and she also took care of the books. However, Will had persistently lectured Chrissy to look for a career beyond the cafe, which had given her the impetus to progress. She had started by doing a short secretarial course that led to temping office work until she landed the job with Waite and Sons.

Waite and Sons was a large top City legal firm run by Jeremy Waite and associated with his son Thomas's Candour group of companies. The Candour group and Waite and Sons were located in Holborn in the Candour building, which was named after the company that headed all of Thomas's various enterprises. Thomas was a world-renowned entrepreneur. Chrissy would see him infrequently and would quickly remove herself from his view when she did, as she was painfully shy and quite overcome by the powerful magnetism she felt when she saw him. She always felt so insignificant next to his all-encompassing presence and the crowd of people who seemed to follow him. It was not uncommon for photographers to wait outside the offices when there were newsworthy mergers or business acquisitions that Thomas's companies were making. It seemed that Thomas had a hand in many areas of retail such as ownership of Waite's department stores in various south-east towns, several sports brands, and he had recently acquired a top menswear brand.

Thomas was taller than most men with broad shoulders and what Chrissy imagined were a rippled abdomen and flat stomach. She felt herself blush as she thought of him now. He was always so immaculately dressed, always a white shirt with a three-piece suit and a tasteful silk tie.

Waite and Sons' main client was Candour group and the firm also housed a small criminal department that was headed by Nicholas, Mr Waite's youngest son. Chrissy worked at first for the commercial arm of the firm in the administration department and post. Nicholas would come down quite often and came to know Chrissy, and he arranged for her to do some work in the criminal department. Her workload changed from typing to casework as Nicholas was able to delegate more and more work to her.

On obtaining her job Chrissy could pay the limited household costs and tried not to touch the few thousand pounds left of her share of her parents' money. Will wouldn't take rent from her even when she started full-time work for Waite and Sons, saying he had got a bargain when he had purchased her parents' business; he joked that to take rent from her would lead to Chrissy's parents coming back to haunt him, and at his age he couldn't handle this. She would hear from Anne maybe once a year if that – but little did they know that life was about to throw them another curveball.

Chrissy had been existing in relative comfort before Nico was born. She had considered that this was to be her life, but with the advent of Nico's birth there grew a passion and power to love a tiny form and the desire to achieve a greater stability for him. Her goal became to strive to give him all her parents had provided for her and Anne.

Chrissy wasn't too sure who Anne's date was tonight. Anne had told her that he was nobody Chrissy would know and he was someone who wanted to spoil her. Anne had a little devious smile on her lips as she said this and Chrissy could not help but feel anxious. Chrissy sighed, bringing her attention back to this contented moment as she nudged her body closer to Nico and breathed in the scent of his hair – those baby smells they both had after his evening bath and their obligatory powder fight.

Just before going to sleep, Chrissy and Nico had knelt beside their bed to send a message to his father. 'Hi, Dad, it's Nico again. I hope you are OK. Mama said you saw me use the big slide today. It was a little bit scary but I really liked it. I had five goes on it. I love you, goodnight.' Nico got to his feet and kissed his fingers, gently touching them to the lips on the photo of Nicholas that stood on their bedside table. This was the ritual that had developed over the years. Chrissy considered that it was important for Nico to have a connection with Nicholas. The park adventures this afternoon had left him exhausted and asleep within five minutes of starting to read a favourite storybook about a gang of heroic dogs.

The sound of soft music playing permeated her ears again and she wondered what Anne and her date were doing. They had been out to dinner and were in their shabby lounge. Chrissy then heard footsteps pass her room and a deep voice as Anne's date passed their room, presumably going to the bathroom. Chrissy closed her eyes in embarrassment as she imagined the bathroom which though kept spotlessly clean was very old and had a leaking tap and damp patches growing over the bath. The door closed and locked and Chrissy craned her ears to hear the footsteps return. That was her last thought before sleep engulfed her.

Somewhere, someone was shouting. What was all that racket and why was it was suddenly cold? Chrissy tugged to pull the coverings over herself and Nico instinctively, but there was resistance as if someone were holding on to it. Chrissy opened one eye and saw a man standing there holding their coverings up towards him and glaring at her, then at Nico and then Anne in quick succession.

Anne was shouting at the man at the top of her voice. 'How dare you, Thomas!'

'What? What?' His gaze darted from Chrissy to Nico and back again, and then there was a lightbulb moment when his eyes seemed to find an answer, and he was taken aback. 'Chrissy?' He whispered and then looked to Nico again. 'This is Nicholas's child!' There was no doubt in his tone. 'How could you keep him from us?' he accused Anne and Chrissy. 'And why is Chrissy here?' he asked Anne. Then turning to Chrissy, he asked, 'What are you doing here?'

'This is my home, and Anne is my cousin!' Chrissy replied, thinking how ludicrous it was that she had to justify her presence in her own home.

Chrissy's eyes begun to adjust to the light and her gaze fixed on Thomas. Thomas – here, in her home. What was he doing here? She asked herself the same question he had asked her. This wasn't making sense. Was she dreaming? She shivered; she was cold – no, it wasn't a dream, was it? She hadn't seen him in more than five years. Thomas eyed Chrissy intently. He shook his head as if to shake the picture out of his mind, as Nico stirred and moaned. This was no dream.

'You have no right to come in here,' Anne shouted at Thomas.

Her words tailed off as Thomas exhaled and burst out, 'I have every right! Every right, Anne – this is Nicholas's child. You've strung me along for weeks with 'something about Nicholas I ought to know". He mimicked Anne's voice. 'And little did I know that you'd hidden his child from us – we are his family too!'

'Well, he is my son and possession is nine tenths of the law!' Anne spat out the American phrase at Thomas. Chrissy rolled her eyes to the heavens and watched on, rapidly adjusting her nightshirt downwards as nobody seemed to care or notice that it had ridden up to her waist. It was then that she registered Anne's words in horror. Anne hadn't told Nicholas's family about Nico! How could she! Clearly, Anne wanted to get some kind of advantage from Thomas, but what? Chrissy looked down at Nico. He looked like a miniature of his father, with the same dark bouncy curls and deep complexion with dark brown eyes framed against long eyelashes. He also had dimples, which accentuated his angelic features.

'Please,' Chrissy begged, looking from Anne to Thomas. 'Please be quiet and leave the room; Nico will wake up. I won't have him frightened whatever the case – leave this instant.'

Thomas seemed about to contradict her but snapped his head back and nodded at her in agreement. Anne huffed and turned to leave the room as Thomas followed silently behind her.

Chrissy remembered when Anne had met Nico's father, Nicholas, five years ago. Chrissy had already been working at Waite and Sons for four years as a caseworker. Nicholas worked on defending white-collar crimes and some pro bono work for clients who could not afford to fund their cases and who were not eligible for legal aid. Chrissy would handle her own caseload of this pro bono work. She worked well with Nicholas and she had found him to be intelligent and down to earth, yet quite carefree. He was a young man who did not have to worry about whether his department made a profit or broke even, as this was just one of the types of projects ('Cinderella work', as they called it) that seemed to be Nicholas's calling and which Thomas supported through the Candour group.

Chrissy had gradually become involved in assisting Nicholas in his criminal work, often being called in to attend to clients and taking instructions at the office and prison visits, gradually beginning to manage cases herself. She loved the work and despite working often with criminals she found they were some of the most honest people she had ever had met.

Chrissy had always thought it was important to be calm and clear in communications and Nicholas had complimented her work for its precision and thoroughness. They worked well as a team and Chrissy ran the criminal department when Nicholas was away. She would rarely encounter Thomas and, at most, they would exchange a nod as they passed. Mr Waite, however, would stop her when she was in reception and engage in conversation with her, often seeking her out just for an opinion on staff matters and needs. He had first asked her into his office

14

for a welcome 'talk' as senior partner with the firm and Nicholas had said not to be nervous, he just wanted to get to know his new member of staff. This had been true and she found the talk helpful.

Then over the years, it became a custom to meet with Mr Waite every last Thursday of the month so he could be updated with the criminal department's caseload and billing. Chrissy actually looked forward to these meetings in his office, which was on the tenth floor of the building and had a beautiful view over the city. His room was in a mahogany decor with a huge array of law books and statutes on one wall and the other was set with a leather Chesterfield settee and armchair with a coffee table. In the middle of the room was a large desk with papers in organised chaos all over it. His secretary would often come in tutting about the state of the desk and then sent packing once she became too vocal.

Their conversations would stray into their personal lives and Chrissy knew Mr Waite often worried about the happiness of his sons and wanted them to settle down. For what it was worth, Chrissy confirmed to him that Nicholas seemed very happy in his work and lately had been enjoying Anne's company. He was, though, uneasy about not being able to tell if Thomas was happy and Chrissy agreed that she would have no idea either. She thought to herself that Thomas had everything one could desire, so she couldn't imagine that he was unhappy. He was as rich as Midas, had a beautiful London home and an array of glamorous women to adorn his arm, if the magazines were to believed.

Mr Waite had disclosed that Thomas was his son from his first marriage and that his first wife had died of cancer. He had married again a year later to Joanne; she had helped raise Thomas, and then they had Nicholas. Thomas had rebelled as a teenager, having been expelled from school numerous times, and then left school to work in a petrol garage before traveling to China where he had lived for three years. Mr Waite's voice would resound with pride as he would describe how Thomas had then begun to import shoes from China and, slowly, he had grown the

Candour group into the multi-billion enterprise it was today, spreading its tentacles into numerous other areas of business. Waite and Sons had initially been a small commercial firm that dealt with Thomas's fledgling business needs but had exponentially mushroomed as the Candour group had grown. Thomas had then taken on Waite and Sons, in which Mr Waite and Nicholas had a controlling interest. What was clear was Mr Waite's pride in both his sons.

Mr Waite and Chrissy's conversations would generally be about the differences in generations of people and life in general. They would share tea and coconut macaroons, which they discovered they both loved. Then Nicholas had met Anne purely by chance as she had come to the office to collect Chrissy's flat keys, having lost her own. She and Nicholas and had quickly become an item. This aroused media interest in them due to their connection to Thomas, which Anne basked in, and benefited from, as it had brought a lot of modelling contracts her way. Mr Waite and Chrissy would not discuss Anne and Nicholas's budding romance, but both acknowledged that the pair were getting very close.

The brothers, Nicholas and Thomas, were very different; Nicholas was playful and talkative, while Thomas was quieter and aloof, always an observer, and only cracking a smile on rare occasions. Both had thick black hair inherited from their respective mothers, whereas old Mr Waite, their father, had more Viking colouring and sharp features. Thomas had his father's hawkish good looks but surprisingly had inherited his mother's blue eyes. Mr Waite had said Thomas and his mother's eye colour resulted from his mother's Celtic ancestors, whereas Nicholas was boyishly handsome, taking his brown eyes from his mother.

Anne and Nicholas had hit it off immediately after Nicholas had sweet-talked her. The relationship was exciting for Anne, especially given the compliments, flowers and luxurious living he afforded her from their very first meeting. For once Anne seemed attached to someone as she had never been to Chrissy or even Jay or Kim. Anne had always been spoiled by Chrissy's parents as she had in effect been abandoned by her mother, and they wanted her to feel as equally loved as Chrissy. They had also been trying for a child for the first five years of their marriage and here was a beautiful little blonde-haired girl, Anne, a year old, left for them to care for. She had been a gift to them.

Jay's grandparents had been of mixed Indian heritage while Kimberley's roots were in London. Together they were a blend of all that was beautiful in their races. Jay was stern but loving and by looks dark and ruggedly handsome, while Kimberley was a gentle soul with a pale complexion, stunning with long blonde hair and blue eyes. They had met when Jay was employed by Kim's father as a waiter at his cafe. Kim's parents were kind to him, and Kim and Jay fell in love. Jay became like a son to Kim's parents and after they married it was a given that Kim and Jay would inherit the cafe, which they eventually did when Kim's father died. Her parents were made for each other. Kim was very delicate and did not work. She looked after Jay and then Anne and, of course, then Chrissy had come along four years after Anne had been living with them. Jay doted on Kim and looked after her as if she was made out of glass. They would hold hands when they went out or were even sitting at home and radiated a warmth that Chrissy still missed.

'No' was a word that Anne had never been accustomed to, even by the time Chrissy was born. Both girls were the opposite of the other in looks. Anne took after her mother and Kimberley, with her fair English rose complexion and blonde hair, and sharp, striking aquiline features, while Chrissy's heritage would be guessed as Latin with her black hair, Mediterranean complexion and softly flowing features and her father's chocolate-brown eyes. Nobody would have guessed that Anne and Chrissy were related, so little was the resemblance between them.

Their natures too were poles apart. Anne had been the daring sister always taking risks and doing things on the fly, thinking primarily of herself, whereas Chrissy would plan and take calculated steps towards an outcome beneficial to them all, with little in the way of risks.

Of course, when Anne met Nicholas, he pandered to her every whim and continued to spoil her, both of them taking risks – including the one that produced their delightful Nico. Nicholas would tell Chrissy about their regular outings to the theatre, dinner or events, and Anne pretty much moved into his apartment a couple of weeks after they met, which led to Chrissy seeing a lot more of her at the office. Anne seemed very content. There were no plans for the future; they were just content being carried along on a wave, which was how Anne generally lived.

It seemed Nicholas had become obsessed with Anne and vice versa. They were inseparable and a whirlwind romance had ensued. As much as Nicholas was enthralled by Anne, his family did not seem so enamoured with her. Anne always referred to Thomas as the Mad Bull, as she said he would snort as he walked past her in reception when she would be waiting for Nicholas. Anne only encountered Mr Waite once or twice and he had been cordial to her.

Chrissy would go to work and often bought work home with her. It was advantageous that she could type, as she was able to draft applications and statements at home and email them to clients for approval. Chrissy was a homebody; she used to thank the powers that be every night for allowing her this little flat that was her safety, security and serenity, where she would return and lay down the problems of the day and rest.

Chrissy extricated herself from Nico and slipped out of bed. She couldn't avoid Anne and Thomas indefinitely. It was so cold. She reached for her fluffy pink nightgown, warm gratitude flooding her features as she glanced at Nico, before leaving the bedroom. He was so beloved, born in such tragic circumstances. Clearly, Thomas looked furious this evening. Chrissy had not had any interaction with Nicholas's family once Nico had been born as she had resigned from her job to be a mother to Nico. Anne had said that Nicholas's family did not want anything to do with her or her child, and that was case closed – or so Chrissy thought.

18

It had always hurt her that Nicholas's family did not care for Nico and the impact that this would have on Nico growing up, as he would be curious and he would have to be told. How could one not love Nico? Thomas's reaction threw Anne's contentions up in the air now as Chrissy remembered Thomas's fury at seeing Nico.

CHAPTER TWO

nne had become pregnant three months into her relationship with Nicholas. Both had been equally shocked, which was surprising as both were fairly intelligent beings. Chrissy saw that Nicholas had been somewhat distracted at work the day after Anne had told him of her pregnancy. While instructing her regarding a witness statement that had come in from the prosecution, he kept losing his train of thought. She had taken pity on him and nodded her head, thinking she should be able to peruse the evidence herself without a steer.

It became apparent to Chrissy that Anne saw her pregnancy as a means by which she could snag Nicholas in the long term, as their relationship had seemed to be a novelty one that may not have stood the test of time. Anne certainly had never expressed a desire to become a mother, but when it happened, she was aware of how it could be turned to her advantage. She began to appeal to Nicholas and his sense of what was right; he seemed to be coming around to the idea of making a life with Anne, and they discussed marriage and having the baby. Then, four months into the pregnancy, Nicholas had been in a car accident.

Chrissy had been with Mr Waite in one of their monthly meetings. Mr Waite had just leaned forward to pick up a macaroon when Thomas burst into the office. He had run his hand through his hair and looked like he had aged ten years. Chrissy had never seen him so lost and almost shaky. He knelt by his father's chair, took his hand, and almost whispered, 'Dad.' He started and then had to stop. Thomas's loss of composure started to make Mr Waite anxious. Thomas began again. 'Nicholas has been in an accident, Dad, it's very serious – we need to go to the hospital.' Mr Waite leaned back into his seat as if winded, unmasked fear in his eyes, and then suddenly rose, holding Thomas's arm, and Thomas guided him from the room. Chrissy muttered support and followed them into the lift and out to the street level where Thomas's security detail was waiting with the car. Thomas had given her a blank look before following his father into the car.

Chrissy called Anne, who had not heard about the accident. She was understandably upset and making her way to the hospital. Chrissy had gone to the hospital after hours and sat with Mr Waite, Thomas, and Mrs Waite, who had arrived too. They were in the waiting room with members of other patients' families. Chrissy felt that this was a room where they may hear very bad news. It was as if the walls had been coloured that soft shade of blue to soften the screams and cries that would be voiced here, or as if the painting of a calm sea hung on its walls would engulf the anguish that would flow from the bereaved hearts of the room's occupants.

Thomas would give Chrissy the odd nod throughout their time there and she watched as he comforted Mr and Mrs Waite as each hour passed. Anne had sat apart from them and so Chrissy would go and sit with her from time to time. Thomas's security detail, Jesse and Ryan, were providing a steady stream of coffees and teas as the family waited nervously for any news. Each member of medical staff who passed by were probed for information, but all they said was that numerous procedures were being undertaken to save Nicholas. They were under no illusion that Nicholas's life hung in the balance. The doctors and nurses had worked hard to save Nicholas, but to no avail. He had died, and the room cloaked their grief.

'Nicholas's funeral.' Chrissy mused that these two words, even today, sounded alien in the same sentence. The funeral was a very sombre affair, as it should be – he was a young man full of life who had been struck down in his prime. The gathering was a sea of black with a splash of calla lilies sitting on his coffin as many wept for him. Anne had dressed in widow's weeds. Mr and Mrs Waite, their sadness reaching the very depths of their souls, carried themselves with dignity and humility, thanking everybody who attended the funeral. Thomas stood next to Mrs Waite, holding her elbow for support, the expression in his eyes blank and unreadable. Anne was affronted that there had been no offer for her to sit with the family, but she had never tried to get acquainted with them, so she sat with Chrissy and the office staff and friends.

Anne had wanted to abort the baby after Nicholas had died but Chrissy begged for her to keep it. Chrissy was all for individuals making their decisions without judgment, but she felt so much that this child should come into the world. Chrissy felt a selfish need for Anne's child deep within herself. Chrissy had promised that she would bear all responsibility for the baby once it was born. Surprisingly, Anne held her to it. Chrissy was Nico's mother for all intents and purposes, and Anne would just sign on the dotted line for any formalities such as jabs and registration.

Anne had explained to Chrissy that she had spoken to Thomas about her pregnancy, and he had expressed that whether she decided to keep the baby or not was her affair – the family would not be involved. Chrissy had asked Anne intermittently whether Nicholas's family should be made aware that she had decided to keep the baby, and Anne stated that Thomas had made it clear that the family wanted nothing to do with the baby, so that had been the end of that discussion and Chrissy had no reason to doubt it.

Chrissy had been there at Nico's birth and was the first to hold him. Anne never showed any interest in him and there was never any maternal bond as she had made herself absent as soon as she had rested. Anne refused to breastfeed him, so Chrissy had stayed in the hospital with Anne for three nights after Nico was born. Chrissy had become mother and father to Nico, who had been premature and had to be fed through a tube in his nose; this disturbed Chrissy, but Anne paid no heed.

Nico had also required readmission into hospital for jaundice. Although Anne would be present when necessary, there was no pull to mother-hood, and Chrissy did not push it. Chrissy would metaphorically leave doors open for Anne to take control over Nico's immunisations and the like, but she would bow out. Anne did not display any malice towards Nico, but she was absent to him even while being in the same room. Anne had expressed that Nico refer to her as an aunt, but Chrissy had drawn the line and insisted that Anne be recognised by Nico as his mother. Anne agreed, but only if Chrissy too would be known as his mother. So, it transpired that Nico called Anne Mum and Chrissy was Mama. Nico knew that Anne had given birth to him and that she was special, but Chrissy would be there for all his needs.

Even naming him had fallen to Chrissy, who had chosen a name to reflect Nicholas.

Chrissy raised Nico to be grateful for everything. As Nico would always say in his four-year-old's adult voice, 'We are very lucky, Mama.' Even though Anne had given birth to Nico, the deal was that he was Chrissy's son, which was a gift for Chrissy.

Chrissy had handed in her resignation three months before Anne's due date. Mr Waite had tried to persuade her to stay, but she couldn't. She worked just two months of her notice period as Mr Waite had allowed her to leave a month early in lieu of holiday owed. This had worked perfectly as Nico was born early. Chrissy had been catapulted into motherhood and, although she had purchased some baby clothes and a Moses basket to take Nico home in, she quickly acquired the other necessities. Chrissy still had a few thousand pounds of savings and some of her parents' money. Anne contributed very little aside from a few groceries. As Nico turned one, Will asked Chrissy to take over management of the cafe, as he did not want to be there running it himself. This fitted in nicely and, with the help of a baby monitor and the two staff at the cafe, Chrissy was able to meet all of Nico's needs. Mo, the chef, and waitress Sandy were very supportive of her and Nico. This life was enough for Chrissy.

As Chrissy walked down the corridor to the lounge she was at a loss where to begin with Thomas. As it happened, Thomas got up from the threadbare sofa as Chrissy entered the room and Anne turned away from the window she had been looking out of. Domino, their black and white cat, raised her head, gave a little yawn, and buried her head in her paws, quickly going back to sleep without a care in the world. Chrissy turned to Anne and asked, 'What is happening here, Anne?'

Anne pouted. 'They didn't deserve to know.'

Chrissy now registered just what Anne had done. 'But you said that Nicholas's family did not want to have anything to do with Nico!'

'You are a liar!' Thomas boomed.

'Well, what difference does it make? They know now!' Anne spat out at Chrissy, and directing a venomous look at Thomas, who once again seemed about ready to tear Anne apart.

Chrissy put a hand up to Thomas, and he recoiled as if burned, shouting, 'I wouldn't touch her!'

Chrissy tried to get them to reduce the volume as she was sure that their neighbours could hear the commotion.

It wouldn't help to corner Anne, so Chrissy licked her lips, which suddenly felt dry, and turned to Thomas, saying in a conciliatory tone, 'I thought you all knew – I am so sorry that Anne didn't tell you about Nico, and of course if you wish to have a relationship with him you must, and I will do everything to assist, but...'

'What?' Anne began almost apoplectic with rage, her eyes almost bulging out of their sockets, and she began to look quite ugly.

'No buts,' said Thomas, stopping Anne in her tracks. 'She –' he pointed at Anne – 'has denied my family a relationship with a living link to

24

Nicholas. How did I not know that you were related to Chrissy?'

Anne took a step towards Thomas and spat back, 'That's none of your business, is it?'

As she spoke, the doorbell rang. Chrissy was concerned about who it may be. Thomas saw this and said, 'I'll see to it, it's probably Jesse.' Thomas left the room to answer the door and they could hear muffled voices, after which he returned to the lounge. 'Don't worry, it was just Jesse.'

Before either Thomas or Anne could say another word, Chrissy spoke calmly, feeling the need to bring the tone of the conversation down a notch from battle mode. 'Anne is my cousin, but that is irrelevant in the grand scheme of things. Yes, it's true that Nico is Nicholas's son and you should have been made aware of his existence, but he is a young child and we need to be gentle in introducing him to the rest of his family. That is all I want to say.' Chrissy sat back down on the sofa.

Anne walked up to her and held her hand out to her. 'What?' she said. 'I'm his mother, I say who he has a relationship with or not!' She pointed to herself, her anger building as she bunched her hands by her sides into little balls.

'I'm sure the courts will easily dispatch any thoughts you have of keeping him away from us any longer than you already have,' Thomas rasped at Anne, now pacing his little patch of the rug and dragging his fingers through his hair.

This was spiralling out of control, Chrissy thought. She had to neutralise the situation. 'Please,' she appealed, more to Thomas than Anne, who could be very stubborn once she dug her heels in. 'Please trust...' she began.

'Trust? You?' Thomas shouted at Chrissy.

Chrissy flashed an angry expression his way and raised her voice. 'Yes, trust *me*. I have given you no reason not to.' Thomas caught himself before he could retaliate, recognising that this was true. He knew from his father that Chrissy was a straight-shooter and other members of staff thought highly of her.

'I promise you both we will deal with this, recognising what you both want but most importantly knowing what is best for Nico,' said Chrissy.

Anne and Thomas remained quiet; they seemed to have accepted Chrissy's breathing space. Anne sat on a chair in defiant silence and looked out of the window.

Thomas too seemed to calm down as he observed the room he was standing in. It was a tired-looking room with a thick rug covering part of a well-worn carpet and shabby sofa. Thomas expected that money was probably not being spent on the decor as it was screaming for a fresh lick of paint and probably scaffolding if the cracks in the corridor and lounge were anything to go by. That said, there was a spirit in this room, the walls of which held photos of Nico alone and with Chrissy and a couple who were probably Chrissy's parents. There were no toys here, though, Thomas observed.

Thomas turned his attention to Chrissy, who sat in silence. He recollected the shock he had got when he had lifted the cover from the bed earlier. In retrospect, he had no right to do that, but he couldn't resist seeing who else was in the flat or what it was Anne seemed to be hiding. Little did he imagine that it was the beautiful woman whom he remembered from mere glances of her at the offices before she had vanished. He had resolved not to pursue her for fear of frightening her away five years ago. He had not expected that her allure would still be capable of tempting him. She was as stunning as he remembered her. He could not imagine how anybody would not agree that Chrissy was one of the most beautiful women they had ever seen. He certainly did. Strangely her scent was also ingrained in his psyche and it was a welcome recognition to have once again sensed her again. He must be quite mad, he thought.

He shook his head for the umpteenth time this evening. What was he thinking? That child, so obviously Nicholas's child, had knocked him for six, as had the vision of Chrissy. He banished outrageous thoughts of Chrissy from his mind and willed himself to listen to her even though the words were spilling from luscious pink lips that he could imagine ravishing. His desire for her was as alive as it had been five years ago, and it pulsated through every vein in his body as she stood up to gain some confidence and adjusted her too-short nightgown. He tried to concentrate on her words, her solemn look turning him to mush. He couldn't trust himself to open his mouth at present so he stayed silent. He found he couldn't think straight.

'Thomas, I will discuss this with Anne and I will contact you, OK?' Chrissy looked from Anne to Thomas, Anne raising her chin in defiance and Thomas nodding. With that, he moved towards the exit of the flat. Chrissy walked behind him, stopping at the hall table to pick up a pen and a pad of post-it notes. She quickly scrawled her mobile number and name and handed it to Thomas as he left the flat and turned back to her. 'It's my number,' Chrissy said. He took a card from his wallet and handed it to her, nodding and leaving. Chrissy closed the door and sighed in relief.

As Chrissy walked back to the lounge, her mind strayed to how handsome Thomas had looked tonight – tall and imposing in his expensive sleek suit. He had one of those faces that drew admiring glances, with his dark hair and startling blue eyes that were a shock to the senses as they were framed by long dark lashes. He was the cliché of tall, dark and handsome. Rich, too, she reminded herself – too rich for her in every way. Chrissy forced herself out of her reverie as she approached Anne and dragged in a long breath.

'Anne, we have to let Nico get to know Nicholas's family,' Chrissy began, ready for a battle – but all of a sudden there was no fight from Anne.

'What do I care, anyway? He is your son for all intents and purposes,' Anne replied.

'Don't be like that, Anne,' Chrissy reasoned. 'We can all be happy with this...'

'I'm not interested,' said Anne, exasperated. 'You handle it, but don't look to me for any support when it all falls apart,' she flung back over her shoulder as she left the room.

'Wow,' Chrissy sighed. 'That's it, it's all on me now.' Sleep began to pull at her eyelids as she walked to her room. Nico was still sound asleep. That child could sleep through an avalanche and then wake if a pin dropped. It was the nature of all children, just like being taken to the doctor with a cough, and then not coughing once when being seen. Children often made liars of parents! Chrissy quietly snuck under the quilt without allowing any air to escape from the warm cocoon that ensconced Nico; she snuggled closer to him and let the heat from his body infiltrate her cold bones.

How would she deal with the introduction of Nico to Nicholas's family? Growing up, Nico had asked why he didn't have a dad, and Chrissy had told him that his father was in heaven. His young mind had not moved on to the thoughts of an extended family or grandparents, so at least there would not be any backtracking needed. Chrissy was always amazed at Nico's capacity to adapt to change and accept people, looking for only good in people. Chrissy had alerted him to his own instincts regarding situations and people, as well as teaching him about stranger danger. She didn't know whether the decisions she would make would be the right ones, but she felt surprisingly calm and instinctively knew that what she was doing was right for Nico.

The dynamics in this situation had changed. She and Thomas would need to be on the same page and do what was right for Nico. The shyness she would feel around him in the office needed to be put aside as she was not in this situation for herself but as Nico's Mama. Yes, it was all about Nico now, and she felt Thomas would have this focus too. With this, her thoughts began to fade and her eyes closed to welcome sleep.

CHAPTER THREE

*T*homas stood on the metal staircase outside Anne's flat. It was a cold, crisp night and it had just rained. There were puddles everywhere but he didn't feel the cold. He felt rejuvenated. He was still in shock. Nothing could have prepared him for this. Why didn't he know that Anne and Chrissy were related? He dredged his memory back through the past to try to remember any mention of Chrissy and Anne being related but could not find any. Did Chrissy hide this and was there a sinister plot? He felt sure Chrissy would not be involved in such a deception. Also, why had Anne hidden Nico's existence from them? It just wasn't making much sense and he couldn't find answers.

Due to his exposure in the press and his financial worth he always had to travel with a security detail, and his relationship with his men was one of respect and loyalty that ran both ways. Jesse and Ryan travelled everywhere with him. As Thomas sauntered down the metal staircase, Jesse walked towards him with an umbrella and walked back to the car, opening the limousine door for him. As he was cushioned into the soft warmth of the heated seats he pondered over the time since Nicholas had died. Life had gone on but like a shell of its former self. He was like a man searching for something nameless, something that was missing and made him very much incomplete. Since Nicholas's death, that feeling had come to the fore; he had sought to develop better ties with his mother and father, and ensure that their remaining life was as stress-free as he could make it. Yes, he had money and a lifestyle many would envy, but he wanted more – but what exactly that 'more' was evaded him.

It was true that Thomas and Nicholas were step-siblings but they had never seen it that way. Jo had been the only mother he had known, since she had married his father when Thomas was just over two years old, and she had been kind to him. Nicholas had been his only sibling and was younger than him by five years. There wasn't a day that went by when Thomas didn't miss him or ask, 'Why Nicholas?' He would happily have traded places with him and been the one to perish. Nicholas was the best of them both, the happiest and the one who enjoyed life the most. Thomas felt he and Nicholas had not spent enough time with each other as adults. He reflected on how strange it was that work and other commitments separated a person from the everyday lives of those closest to them – then one day it was too late and they were gone. Anne had offered what seemed like a link to Nicholas, something more of Nicholas, but little did he know how great this link would be. He smiled beyond the bitterness of being deprived knowledge of Nico's existence and was thankful for this gift that he would share with his parents. He was also very pleased that the wrapping that Nico came in would be Chrissy, whom he intended to weave into the fabric of his life.

It had been more than a month ago that he had run into Anne as he was about to step into his car after a meeting with the bank. He had almost walked past her as she put a hand out to pull at his elbow. He stopped and recognised her. She had been Nicholas's girlfriend when he had met with an accident and died. She was an unpleasant woman who had taken him to one side to try to blackmail him into paying her off, or she would publish intimate photos of her and Nicholas in the press. Thomas had been furious and had dared her to do so, making it clear that the only place she would go to if she was serious would be prison, as his security people had witnessed this blackmail attempt and would attest to this to the police.

She had disappeared quick-smart after that. He tried to sidestep away from her, but she had stopped him in his tracks. She said that she felt he ought to know something about Nicholas, but she wasn't convinced he deserved to know. She had warned him that if he made any threats to her or pushed her, she would make sure he never found out. She could be bluffing, but something inside him willed him not to take the risk. They made civil chit-chat but she would not be drawn on the subject further. His gut told him that he needed to talk to her, and hence his connection with Anne had begun. There was never anything romantic between them; Anne was trying to tempt him, but failing miserably. Thomas was just committed to finding out what information she had on Nicholas.

Anne had thus far strung Thomas along to a dinner and a gallery opening on the promise she would disclose what she knew, but she had never seemed to trust that she should tell him. He had wondered why she had taken him to that dilapidated flat, and now he knew why. Of course, he had found out the secret himself, but why was she furious? Surely she had brought him to the flat to show him. So, Nicholas had a child, the spitting image of his brother when he was young, and obviously named after him. For this, he felt a joy he couldn't name. A part of Nicholas was alive, was here, and his parents would be overjoyed. He determined that Nico would know this side of the family and enjoy any benefits this could confer on him. He could certainly massively improve the standard of his life.

Chrissy was the way to a relationship with Nico. Thomas could not have thought of a more amiable route than her. He had always thought of her as possessing a rare type of beauty that also radiated wholesome goodness. This is the only way he could describe it. In a high-powered world of sharp and harsh posturing, she gave off a softness and honesty that was so rare. He knew that his father and Chrissy had a good rapport, but Thomas had never made a move to get to know her as he was sure he would frighten her off and he did not want to complicate her life. It was a different ball game now and he was about to complicate the hell out of her life. Nature had put her in his path for a reason and that was a green light enough for him.

Thomas recalled that Chrissy had handed in her notice shortly after Nicholas had died and had never really explained why other than saying her departure was for 'personal reasons'. Thomas and his father had decided to keep the criminal department open in homage to Nicholas as it had been important to him. In her remaining time with the firm, Chrissy had assisted in the selection of head of the criminal department and also her replacement. He knew Mr Waite missed her and, of course, Mr and Mrs Waite both missed Nicholas dreadfully.

Nicholas's death had changed many things, but none more so than Thomas's lifestyle. It had been full of regular engagements for charity and industry, and there would be a stream of glamorous women to adorn his arm and warm his bed. He was after all a virile man with a healthy appetite and bank balance so the ladies were well looked after both before and after any connection with him ended. He found that the women he encountered were clear about what they wanted from him, and he managed to extricate himself easily once their mutual needs were fulfilled. He couldn't say he had had a relationship with a woman as there had not been anyone with whom he had wanted to make conversation, wake up to or idly lie in bed. He had also not been one to sleep in as there had always been some meeting or event to attend.

With Nicholas's passing, the need to attend events had been effectively delegated to Thomas's various heads of departments. Even his living accommodation had changed. He found himself reprioritising life and making a reality his wish to spend more time with his parents. Although he wanted to maintain his personal space, he also wanted to be on hand for them in the future. He had fielded the idea of his parents moving into his house in the City but he could see it would be a wrench for them to leave their home in the quiet of Surrey, and that they would be torn between being close to their only remaining son and living in the home that they loved. Thus it was agreed that Thomas would move in with them and have their home extended, which led to it doubling in size. This was a better plan for his parents and for him, he thought.

Two extra wings had been added to either side of the house so that it did not detract from the symmetry of the property. The kitchen was extended and had a door leading into a large conservatory, which in turn led into the garden through huge patio doors. The main entrance door opened into a domed foyer that resembled an enormous regal conservatory scattered with potted palms and majestic cascading flowering plants, with rising columns of marble trimmed with chrome. The main path led from the main door to all the rooms on the ground floor and also split into various secluded areas where couches and love seats were scattered. There was a family seating area where his parents could frequently be found with friends, or alone reading or relaxing with a game of Scrabble or some such activity. They tended to call this section the garden room. The dome reached up to the top of the main staircase, so providing as much natural daylight as the weather would allow. This feature had been a surprise for his mother, who had loved this decor at her favourite hotel in town.

The main staircase split in the middle toward the two wings. Most of the house was decorated in apricot, cream and silver, save for the blue room. There were two staircases from the kitchen and one main staircase leading to the upper floor. A gym was added with a swimming pool, Jacuzzi, steam, sauna and changing rooms. An outdoor tennis court was built too, as his mother and father loved playing tennis. His mother's rose gardens were also extended and landscaped to her taste and requirements, and his father's small patch of vegetable garden was enlarged to a huge allotment with a large shed.

Their lives also settled into some routine whereby they made sure that they saw each other most mornings and evenings, which led to more talking and sharing even the most mundane events of the day. They laughed a lot more and in a way Nicholas's death had brought them closer to each other. Life at the office had also changed for Mr Waite, who retired to spend more time with his wife, and another senior partner had been made managing partner.

Work life for Thomas had remained as demanding as ever, but he had little to no interaction with the criminal department himself. When Chrissy had been there, he used to make excuses to pass by and hover over paperwork in the receptionist's out tray in the hope of catching a glimpse of her. However, he had never had the opportunity to watch her at his leisure. He had been struck by her sultry beauty the first time he had seen her in her no-nonsense office clothes. She had been wearing a grey suit with a fitted pencil skirt that sculpted her beautifully formed bottom and led to a small slit that allowed a glimpse of her shapely legs and narrow ankles ensconced in sensible brogues. Those feet should have been clad in red high heels, he had thought. This vision was surpassed by her state of undress this evening, when she had been clad only in a pink fluffy nightgown that fell to just above her knees, exposing those sexy legs and small bare feet to his clear view. Her hair was a mass of curls falling about her shoulders. Of course, he had got an eyeful earlier when she was half-asleep in bed. Her barely there nightshirt gifted him a look at her shapely sun-kissed body, and her black underwear fitted neatly over her flat stomach and an inviting mound. Her eyes had been dazed with shock and she had flung her hand across her face as she regained her composure.

The car stopped and Jesse opened the door for him. Thomas's mouth curled into a devilish grin as his thoughts mentally untangled Chrissy from her nightgown, leaving her standing before him in all her glory. He was struck by an almost primal reaction and a tightening on his crotch that slowed down his alighting from the car. Snap out of it, he chastised himself, giving himself a mental shake to erase the vision of her.

Though Nico was of the utmost importance, Thomas understood that life had given him another chance to explore Chrissy. He had a feeling she could rock his world and this time he would take the chance and let her.

Surprisingly, Chrissy quickly drifted off to sleep and woke after what felt like just five minutes of sleep, but it was ten o'clock. Nico was under the covers talking to Wombie, his little red and white striped Womble-like soft toy that Chrissy had bought him for his first birthday. He wouldn't go anywhere without it and he would have long discussions with it; about what, nobody quite knew. 'Are you up my lovely,' Chrissy whispered, acknowledging the importance of the discussion being had between boy and toy. 'Shhh, Mama, me and Wombie need to catch Domino,' Nico whispered back. Chrissy stifled a laugh as she imagined the merry dance that would be led when Domino's slippery form would evade boy and toy when they made a futile attempt to try to catch her again.

Domino was evasive, quite unpredictable, and frankly quite selfish, as is the way of cats. She always managed to outwit Chrissy who had sustained many an injury when attempting to load her into the pet carrier to take her to the vet. So, it came to pass that vets' visits would only be possible if Domino were rendered immobile or her movement restricted, which thankfully had not yet happened.

'You should leave her alone,' Chrissy said softly to Nico, trying not to make it sound like a challenge. Chrissy gently got out of bed, leaving the covers still over Nico's head as he sat up, stretching his arms above his head and yawning loudly. Before she knew it, he was up and had grasped her hand, pulling her to the door, Wombie's nose firmly grasped in his other hand.

The kitchen was a bit of a mess, Chrissy thought. Anne would still be in bed. Anne had left her empty bottle of wine on the counter with a half a punnet of strawberries. There were also half-eaten Chinese food containers that Anne must have left before going out for the evening yesterday.

Spillages were all over the counter space. Nico was in the lounge talking away to Wombie as Domino rushed into the kitchen and started to eat her food. Nico sauntered in, eyeing Domino with a sideways glance and whispering to Wombie that they'd catch her later because 'she knows' they want to catch her now. Chrissy grinned, and she could hear Mo and Sandy downstairs in the cafe. The rush must have died down and it was early closing, today being a Saturday. She would go down a little later.

Nico settled at the chair nearest the window overlooking the back of the church next door. He looked down at the church's big bell, which tolled three times a day. 'How long before the bell, Mama?' Nico asked. 'Two hours, darling,' Chrissy replied as she poured milk over Nico's cereal. Nico spooned an imaginary amount of cereal into Wombie's mouth as they both discussed the day ahead.

Chrissy dressed Nico before she could dress as he played on her bed with his interactive bus toy, pressing each alphabet letter as requested and having immense fun. Chrissy pulled on a red T-shirt and jeans. Nico insisted that they both wear red after the clothing of his favourite character in a cartoon about action dogs. Both of them, therefore, had predominantly red wardrobes.

It was a trainers kind of day today, Chrissy thought, as she tied her laces and told Nico to get his. She tied his laces and took his hand as they opened the door leading to the cafe and descended the stairs together, Nico counting each step.

'Hey, Mo,' called Chrissy as she passed the kitchen door. Sandy was taking an order from a customer at the till. A plate was waiting at the pass and Chrissy quickly donned an apron and served the dish. Nico had run into the kitchen to greet Mo, had seated himself at his table behind the counter, and was impressing Sandy with his alphabet now. Sandy laughed as Nico leaped from T to XYZ and nodded at his own genius.

The morning rush had ended and there were only four customers in the cafe, which would close at 2pm today. Chrissy checked in with

Mo and his list of supplies, ensuring that there would be no rush for Monday morning, and noted that there were only a couple of invoices, which she quickly dealt with. She emptied the dishwasher and prepared sets of cutleries to be laid, checked all was for closing and they said their goodbyes. Sandy and Mo would lock up the cafe, which pretty much ran itself, and there wasn't much that Chrissy had to do. Will insisted that she let him sleep well at night knowing that his cafe was in 'safe hands' – i.e., hers. She interrupted Nico's colouring to take him upstairs to pack his swimming kit for his lesson today.

Chrissy followed Nico into their room as she sat on the bed and watched him take his swimming trunks out of his drawer and place them into his rucksack, followed by his towel, and then he plopped himself on the bed with her. She already had her bag packed with her swimming costume and necessities, so they went to the kitchen to prepare a drink and snacks for Nico to demolish after swimming when he was always ravenously hungry. She would take him for lunch at his favourite fast food place this afternoon, which would be a nice surprise.

The leisure centre was busy today with kids and parents rushing to classes and balancing babies. 'Wait for me,' Chrissy shouted as Nico rushed to leave the changing rooms after putting on his trunks. Chrissy quickly closed their locker and pinned the key to her swimming costume, as she walked towards Nico, reiterating 'no running' to him. 'Hello, Nico,' shouted the swimming coach, Amanda, as they quickly walked towards the learners' pool. Nico kissed Chrissy and was gone with a hasty 'Bye, Mama!' He jumped into the pool before she knew what was what, leaving Chrissy to slide into the opposite end of the pool nearby so that she wouldn't get cold and could see how Nico was doing. He was quite a strong swimmer and loved to help other learners practise.

After the session, Nico enthused about how fun it had been as they both showered and Chrissy brushed his hair. He sat patiently in the cubicle, munching on his apple, watching her dry herself and get dressed. Nico had begun to get curious about bodies and Chrissy had to be discreet when dressing to avoid embarrassing questions in public. She dried her hair and they left the swimming baths.

'Are you hungry, baby?' Chrissy asked Nico.

'Yes, Mama, but I'm going to be very hungry soon,' he said knowingly, as he began to open a bag of corn snacks.

'Mama, your phone is ringing,' Nico said, as Chrissy hadn't heard the ring tone. She managed to rummage in her bag for it and answered, halting Nico as he made to speed homeward-bound, intent on dragging her along with him.

She hadn't immediately recognised the number, though the voice was unmistakable. It was Thomas. 'Hi, Chrissy?' he asked tentatively.

'Ah, yes, Thomas, how are you?' Chrissy asked, forcing herself to keep her voice calm, as her heart was jumping about and causing all kinds of havoc with her nerves.

'I'm fine – you and Nico?' he replied.

'Well...!' She trailed off as she turned and caught Nico's eye and smiled. 'We have had the mostest fun swimming, haven't we, Nico?'

'Yes,' he shouted enthusiastically, and Chrissy could hear Thomas chuckling.

'That's good news. I wondered if you haven't had lunch yet, maybe we could meet and have lunch together?'

Chrissy readily agreed, as there was no reason why Nico should not meet his family and lunch was next on their agenda anyway. 'No, we haven't had lunch yet – we could meet, yes,' she replied, without giving her brain the chance to catch up with her mouth.

They agreed that Thomas would pick them up in an hour. Chrissy explained to Nico as they walked back home that they were meeting someone for lunch. It was a new person who wanted very much to meet him. 'Who is it, Mama?' Nico had asked curiously.

'His name is Thomas, Nico. You know Anne is your mum and your dad

38

Nicholas is in heaven – well, Thomas is your dad's brother. He is your uncle!' Chrissy said as they climbed the external stairs to the flat together.

'Is he a real uncle, Mama?' Nico asked sweetly.

'Yes, darling, and you should call him uncle Thomas,' Chrissy explained.

'Will he be able to tell me more about my dad?' Nico asked, pondering this prospective uncle as a well of information about his father.

Chrissy decided to leave it to Thomas to introduce the subject of their parents. It would be nice for Thomas to be that link for Nico and make their bond that much stronger, Chrissy hoped, as she chopped up some carrots for Nico to munch on. She also handed him a little bowl of cat treats for Domino. Nico went into the lounge muttering to Wombie as he settled on the sofa, tempting Domino to snuggle next to him by placing the treats next to him.

There was no sign of Anne, which was not unusual, and Chrissy didn't know what her plans were now that the cat – Nico – was out of the bag. Their lives hardly ever overlapped, let alone collided like last night.

Chrissy hurriedly gathered their wet swimming things and put them into the washing machine before going to her bedroom to freshen up a little, applying a dab of perfume, a plum-colour lipstick, and a little brown eyeliner, which brightened up her face considerably. She studied her face in the mirror; it was heart-shaped with high cheekbones and long eyelashes. Her colouring was a warm brown framed by a riot of dark brown hair. She smiled as she remembered Mo calling her a hothouse flower; she quite liked the way she looked. She wondered what Thomas made of her. Did he even notice her at all? Because she was very aware of him. Of course not, she chided herself. Chrissy had never thought so when she used to work for the firm; he would just give her a passing glance or have his face buried in some papers when she saw him.

39

CHAPTER FOUR

Thomas had reached home late and so had slept in the next morning, which was unusual for him as he was an early riser even on weekends. He lay back on his pillow, surprised that he had slept so well after the shock of discovering about Nico and then also unexpectedly being treated to seeing Chrissy. He smiled as he thought about Chrissy and Nico. She seemed so totally unaware of the magnetism that drew him to her, or how her presence made him want to reach out and touch her. Then there was Nico, whose existence was like a bolt out of the blue. Seeing Chrissy again had ignited a joy within him that seemed to flicker with anticipation and blaze brighter each time he saw her. He would be seeing them today, he would make sure of it. Thomas closed his eyes as he hatched a plot to manoeuvre Chrissy into his day.

The smile lingered and lit up his face as he imagined how his parents would react to being told about Nico, a grandson they never knew they had. With that thought, he bounded out of bed and sauntered down the back staircase to the kitchen.

AJ, Jesse and Ryan all lived in apartments above the kitchen which had separate, private exits at the back of the house. Thomas greeted Jesse and Ryan, who were in the kitchen having breakfast, asking them to be ready to leave in an hour. AJ was at the counter rolling out some pastry as

Thomas passed her and playfully poked her waist with a finger, dazzling her with a smile. AJ, aka Alison Jensen, had been with the family since Thomas had been a toddler. Officially she was the housekeeper but in fact she was a member of the family; she cared for them and they in turn cared for her. She was a bachelor (she refused to be called a spinster), having prided herself on not having 'settled' for a life with a partner when she had not found 'the one'. She said she had the Waites, her nieces, nephews and their respective children, and that was enough for her. AJ was always dressed in a flowery dress or top and trousers with her standard black apron. 'The garden room,' AJ said, as Thomas raised an inquiring brow regarding the whereabouts of his parents.

His mother and father were already wide awake and debating the pros and cons of beekeeping. Mr Waite was very keen, having watched a programme on the extinction of bees and their benefit to nature and the world. Mrs Waite, on the other hand, had no such heroic notions and wisely knew the limitations of her husband's abilities – and neither had the patience or the ability to avoid being stung to death by angry bees.

'Look Jo, I'm just saying think about it!' Mr Waite reasoned.

'No, Jem, I know you better than you know yourself. I won't budge on this – it's not the hobby for you! Find another one,' said Mrs Waite, through firmly pursed lips which were the sign that she meant business and it was pointless trying to move her.

They had eaten breakfast, and Jo was knitting a red cardigan while Jem sat peering into the laptop, reading up on the practicalities of beekeeping. 'Good morning, Tom. Coffee?' called his mother as she got up to pour them both a cup.

'Morning, son,' joined his father.

'Morning, lovely people, and yes to the coffee, Ma,' beamed Thomas, causing Jo to wonder to herself, 'Aha, what's happening here?' She had a mother's a sixth sense when it came to Thomas, and she knew there was a story here, one that he could not wait to tell. AJ had arrived too and looked on, her curiosity aroused.

'Now, sit down, Ma, and AJ – you sit down too.' He beckoned her towards a chair that he had drawn up next to where Jo was sitting on the couch. 'I'll tell you all some fantastic news'. Thomas knew that this would come as a shock to them all, but he could barely compose himself as they all looked at him in anticipation. 'As you know I have been in contact with Anne for a couple of months now,' he began.

Jo and Jem looked at each other in disappointment and AJ just shook her head. Thomas was not usually stupid, which was why they thought he had lost his senses, and they told him so. Surely he was not planning a future with Anne? All their minds were running a mile a minute. 'Now, you're young, Tom, you don't need to make decisions so soon – take your time,' Jo interrupted, afraid of what Thomas was going to say.

Thomas looked at her, astounded. 'What are you talking about?'

'I know I'm always talking about you settling down, but –' Jo sped on.

'I'm not talking about settling down, Ma', Thomas interjected. 'Concentrate on what I say.' Thomas took a chair and placed it next to his parents. He sat down and gently took one of each of their hands in his, as he began to talk again, all the time looking into their eyes.

'Ma, Dad, AJ. Nicholas has a son.' Thomas breathed out.

Jo, Jem and AJ looked at each other at the mention of Nicholas's name, not quite registering what he had said.

'You are grandparents, guys,' said Thomas.

Slowly a fog seemed to be clearing from their minds as if they had seen something they could not quite believe. 'H-how?' asked Jo, shaking whatever mist remained from her mind. 'I mean, tell us, Tom!' she pleaded, turning tearful eyes to meet Jem's, which were also welling up now as each comprehended the enormity of the news that Thomas was relaying. AJ was still reeling; Thomas could see that, as she got up from her seat and then immediately sat back down with her hands in her lap.

'Anne had been telling me that there was some information about

Nicholas that she wasn't sure she should tell me, but I was determined to find out what it was,' Thomas continued. 'I went to her flat yesterday and I discovered that Anne had had Nicholas's baby – he's a little boy now.'

Jem moved to the edge of his seat, and Jo's hand flew to her mouth.

'His name is Nico and he is four years old,' added Thomas, looking from his mother to his father, who both sat riveted.

Thomas turned to his father. 'I also found out that Chrissy is Anne's cousin.' He raised an inquiring eyebrow, as though to ask if this was news to his father.

'Well, I knew that, son, but it didn't seem important – they were both so different...' his sentence petered out.

'Guys, Nico looks just like Nicholas as a child,' Thomas enthused further.

Jo touched her cheeks and then locked hands with Jem. 'We will be able to see him won't we, Tom? I mean, Anne kept him from us. Will she allow it?' she asked nervously, clearly afraid that their miracle would go unseen.

'I'm going to speak to Chrissy today and I am hoping she will be able to persuade Anne that it would be in Nico's interests to let him have a relationship with us.'

Jo was comforted by these words, and brought Jem's hands to her lips and kissed them, her eyes shining with tears of hope and a light that had disappeared with Nicholas.

Jem pressed her hands and held them to his chest, turning to Thomas, saying, 'Son, you go and calm the waters for us. We need to welcome our grandchild, Nicholas's boy.' He turned to AJ for her to share this moment. She had helped raise Nicholas from birth, loving him and then mourning his loss with them when he died. Her eyes were also full of happy tears. 'Tom,' added Jem, 'if Chrissy has any say in this issue, then I am confident that she will make sure that right is done by us.'

Thomas was surprised by his father's faith in Chrissy, and he hoped he was right. Thomas had always been the son in whom the faith was placed to get things done. Nicholas had been the one for whom things were done by all of them with love and care. Just before Nicholas's accident, both sons had truly taken the mantle from their parents so they could relax into their later years by reducing their father's workload. The loss of Nicholas had greatly unsettled them but also then grounded them more firmly, and the pieces of their life at last seemed to be falling into place.

Thomas left them to contemplate meeting Nico, squeezing AJ's shoulder as he left to go to his room.

'Here!' AJ shouted as he turned and expertly caught a peach she had thrown in his direction. 'Breakfast?' AJ asked as he sped away.

'No time to eat, AJ! People to see, nephews to meet!' replied Thomas. He was looking forward to meeting Nico and having a piece of Nicholas back in his life, but something more stirred inside him like a warm promise as he fed the hope that Nico would be accompanied by Chrissy stepping into their lives.

Thomas found the scrap of paper that Chrissy had written her number on and called her from his phone. Chrissy and Nico had been swimming and sounded like they were having fun and were quite giggly. She agreed to meet him for lunch and so Thomas raced into the shower before quickly dressing in casual clothes and descending the main stairs. His mother was at the front door.

She approached him slowly and held out something for him. 'Tom, give this to Nico.' It was Nicholas's old red scarf. He had called it his 'lucky' scarf that he wore on occasions when he felt he needed a boost. After his accident, Jo had kept it in her bedside drawer, and she would take it out and hold it to her nose as if to inhale him again. Thomas nodded.

'Tell him it was his father's lucky scarf and tell him that we want to see him,' she said as Jem joined her and grasped her shoulders in support, nodding at Thomas. Thomas could see the hope in them both. Even though Jem spoke little, he felt just as emotional as Jo.

Ryan was at the front entrance in the black Range Rover while Jesse got out to open the door for Thomas. Thinking Nico would need a safety seat,

Thomas had asked Ryan to arrange for one to be fitted into the back seat next to the other door. There was another spare child seat in the boot just in case. The family needed to be prepared to travel with Nico in various cars. It was a nice feeling, this planning for happy times ahead.

As the car pulled up outside Chrissy's, Thomas looked up at the flat and admitted to feeling a little nervous at the thought of meeting Nico. He had not had much experience interacting with young children, so this was going to be interesting. He walked up the stairs and rang the doorbell, smiling as the chimes played 'Twinkle, Twinkle, Little Star'.

The bell was still chiming as Chrissy went to answer the door, quickly looking at herself in the old mirror that hung in the hall and straightening her top. She called out to Nico, who poked his head around the door frame, holding his faithful Wombie by his nose, and Domino sitting at his feet. Chrissy smiled as she opened the door to Thomas – and to another world of people who would care for Nico and form the village that would, she hoped, help raise him. It was a comforting thought, as up until now she always felt alone in her love for Nico and worried about his care should anything happen to her. Mr Waite was a good man and even if Thomas were half the man he was, then Nico was a lucky boy. Here, standing at their door, was another branch of Nico's family. Thomas greeted her as he entered and his eyes lowered to the red T-shirt that was fitted to her ample breasts and cut a voluptuous shape. Chrissy sounded an 'ahem' and tilted her head towards the lounge as she beckoned Thomas to come in.

He was dressed all in black, from his suede loafers, jeans and shirt to his blazer. Chrissy mulled over how very handsome he was, that shyness she always felt around him rearing its embarrassing head. He was tall and dark and shared the same colouring as her with his black hair, but his piercing blue eyes would always make her heart skip a beat for their clarity and sheer beauty. His chiselled features boasted a Grecian nose and strong cheekbones that gracefully merged into his face and led to a cleft in his chin. His familiar citrus scent permeated the air as he stood, and a cold gust of wind passed him.

Once inside, Thomas turned to face Chrissy. Her dark brown eyes seemed to him to swallow him and drown him in their depths as they smiled back at him. She always had this effect on him and the years without seeing her had not dulled his sense of her. There was a familiar scent to Chrissy that reminded him of fresh peaches. Combined with the effect her presence had on him, she was irresistible to him. Yet resist he had for the years she had worked for them. Thomas watched her as she walked away from him. Her jeans clung to her curves and as she turned, his gaze dropped to her round bottom, which lifted in the middle to form two perfectly formed moons, swaying with each step she took towards Nico.

She half-turned to Thomas and halted to allow him to come to her side as they both approached Nico, who just stood by coyly. Thomas couldn't help staring beyond Chrissy at Nico, those same features as Nicholas but a miniature version, dark curls, a plump face and dimples on each cheek. There was silence as uncle and nephew studied each other.

Chrissy felt like she was an interloper as she spoke to Nico. 'Come on, let's show Uncle Thomas in.'

Nico took Thomas's hand in his and led him to the sofa he had been occupying earlier and bid him to sit next to him, patting the seat. 'Sit here, Uncle Thomas, next to me and Wombie. Don't be afraid of Domino, she might come and sit with us,' said Nico. The cat decided she was going to slide back and forth through Thomas's legs as he sat back on the sofa, still holding Nico's hand. Thomas noted rather large cracks and discolouring of the paint on the walls of the room, as well as the threadbare carpets and shabby furniture, which had been barely noticeable last night. Despite this, there was a warm feeling about this home today and he realised it was because these two were in it.

Thomas spoke gently to Nico, stooping his head to bring it level with his. 'Nico, I am your dad's brother and I'm so very happy to meet you.' He suddenly remembered the scarf and fished it out of his blazer pocket. 'My mother, also your dad's mother, who would be...'

'My Grandma,' Nico supplied with a beaming smile.

'Yes,' said Thomas, placing an affectionate hand on Nico's head. 'Grandma sent you a scarf,' he said, presenting the scarf into Nico's hand.

Nico held his hand out, looking at Chrissy for permission to take it, and she nodded. He ran with it to Chrissy. 'Mama, it's red! Red, Mama!' he said excitedly. He loved it. Chrissy brought Nico back with her and sat on the other side of him while he settled back next to Thomas.

'I know, darling. Do you love it?' she asked, knowing that he did.

'I do, Mama, can I wear it today?' Nico asked.

'Of course,' Chrissy spoke, adjusting it around Nico's neck. She turned to Thomas, explaining earnestly to him that Nico's favourite hero dog character wore red, and red of course was for bravery. Nico solemnly nodded his head in agreement as Thomas looked suitably impressed.

'That's interesting,' Thomas said to Nico. 'Now why don't you call me Uncle Tom?'

Chrissy's lips twitched with laughter and Thomas realised she was ribbing him about the reference to *Uncle Tom's Cabin*. He shrugged his shoulders, smiling back at Chrissy, and said, 'It is what it is, right?'

'So, Nico, did your mama tell you we are going out for lunch? What he would like to eat?'

'Passssstaaa!' Nico shouted, his love for his favourite food clear in every syllable as he jumped up.

'Well, then, pasta it is,' Thomas chuckled, standing up ready for action.

The only Italian restaurants that Thomas ever frequented were swanky city eateries conducive to business lunches and dinners. He didn't know any that were child-friendly or local. It was not a consideration he had had to make in the past and he was totally out of his comfort zone. Chrissy read his thoughts and suggested a local Italian restaurant – and judging by Nico's whoop, it sounded like a favourite of his. Nico described watching the chefs spin the pizzas in the air before catching them, after which they would invite Nico to wash his hands and decorate his pizza under the chef's instructions.

Thomas listened intently. He had never had to interact with children before and whereas previously children had seemed cute, noisy and sometimes annoying, now he felt a responsibility and need to adjust his life to fit the needs of this little boy. Although he had only just met Nico, he felt oneness with him, as if blood had recognised blood.

Chrissy held back a little to allow Nico and Thomas to find their connection and to talk. Nico would have no problem filling in any silence with his thoughts, which he was not shy about voicing. She felt Thomas look to her while talking to Nico, seeking reassurance that he was handling this well, and Chrissy nodded discreetly from time to time, Nico oblivious to this unspoken language between the two adults.

'Aren't we hungry, Nico? Go and get our coats, darling,' said Chrissy.

Nico sprung up and ran into their room, followed by Chrissy as she said to Thomas that they would not be long. Nico put Wombie into the bed before moving the toddler step so he could reach their jackets from the back of their door where they hung. Nico went back to Thomas and presented his coat to him without a word, and he immediately held it out for Nico to shrug into before taking Chrissy's coat from Nico and doing likewise for her as she entered the lounge. Chrissy slipped into the coat, her back to him as she flicked her plaited hair from under the coat, it brushing his face. It was such a simple movement, but it seemed so intimate to Thomas, who was able to breathe in her scent, which was subtle and barely there; it was a smell of freshness rather than the cloying, heavy designer perfumes that currently seemed to be worn by the women he associated with. Chrissy felt his touch lasted a little longer than necessary and did not want Thomas to feel uncomfortable, so she stepped out of the circle of his arms. Just as she did so, Nico grabbed

48

Thomas's hand, ready to leave, so Chrissy opened the door and put out her hand in a flourishing gesture for them to pass like royalty.

Nico giggled and started to fire questions at Thomas about their journey as they descended the stairs. Nico was impressed by the big car. Jesse and Ryan both stood by the vehicle and Thomas introduced Nico and Chrissy to them. Nico put out his hand to shake hands with them. Both men smiled at how grown up this little boy was. 'You should get used to Jesse and Ryan,' Thomas said to Nico and Chrissy, 'they are likely to be round a lot – they are bodyguards.' Chrissy was aware of the security detail that Thomas had with him, but was never quite aware that it was *all the time*. He must have them because he was in real danger, she thought, and this made her quite uneasy, both for Thomas and Nico.

Chrissy was surprised and appreciative that a child seat had been fitted for Nico, and the boy liked the idea of a special seat just for him as Thomas insisted on buckling him up. Chrissy sat next to Nico and Thomas slid in beside her. 'No fidgeting with the door, Nico!' Chrissy instructed gently, swiping his hand away from wandering to the catch at the door.

Chrissy named the restaurant and leisure complex where they were headed, for Jesse to locate as Ryan drove. Nico talked a mile a minute, asking questions hypothetical and real and narrating their everyday lives for Thomas with Chrissy confirming whether it was fact or exaggeration. Thomas helped Chrissy out of the car once parked and Jesse went to undo Nico's seatbelt and lift him out of the car on the other side. As they walked to the restaurant, Jesse and Ryan hung back and followed discreetly.

Their late lunch was proving to be a success with Nico, Chrissy and Thomas conversing easily among Nico's adventure in picking pizza ingredients and the chefs tossing the dough in the air for dramatic effect. Nico then enjoyed doing a colouring book as Thomas and Chrissy conversed. 'Chrissy, I am grateful to you for arranging for me to see Nico – I imagine that Anne would not be so accommodating,' said Thomas. 'Also my parents and I want you to know we will accept whatever arrangement you make for us to see Nico.'

'Thomas...' Chrissy began.

'Please call me Tom,' he said. 'We are to be more than we used to be because of Nico, and my family and I owe you a great debt of gratitude for all you do for him.'

'Nico is my life, Thomas.' He raised an eyebrow and she corrected herself. 'Tom it is! He is my family, but also a part of your family, and it is only right that you have a part to play in his upbringing. I believe that the more people who can love and care for a child the better.'

Thomas wanted to ask her something and hoped it would not offend, but he was curious more than anything else. 'I noticed that Nico calls you Mama.'

'Yes, well, Anne does not feel very maternal, and so I agreed that I would be Nico's mama,' said Chrissy, feeling she had to defend Anne. 'She is so busy with her modelling career, so it's best for Nico. Nico calls her Mum and knows exactly who we each are to him.'

As if on cue, Nico piped up, 'Yes, this is my mama and my mum is called Anne. I came from Anne's tummy. She made me.'

Nico had summed this up as only a child could, which made Thomas smile. 'That's right Nico. So, what shall we have for dessert?'

'Uncle Tom, I would like ice cream, please, how about you, Mama?'

'Oooh, let's see.' Chrissy consulted the dessert menu. Chrissy and Thomas, it transpired, loved chocolate ice cream, whereas Nico was a bubble-gum flavour fanatic.

They decided to go to the local park after lunch. Chrissy sat on a bench next to the swings, watching and laughing as Thomas pushed Nico's swing in the air, and he shrieked, 'Higher!' They could easily be mistaken for an ordinary mum and dad out with their son Chrissy, thought. How would it feel to be Tom's family, to be Tom's wife? She had never dared to imagine this. She expected he would cherish his wife. He would make her the centre of his world. He had proved himself to be a gentle and considerate uncle. Chrissy sometimes longed to be 'the one' for someone. Someone to share sadness, tears, fears and love. Maybe one day. Maybe not, she thought, realistically.

Thomas found being in Chrissy's presence soothing and felt perfectly at ease with her and Nico. She was so peaceful just being and even sitting in silence without the need to chatter as if she were drinking in the atmosphere with all her senses. She also had a refreshing honesty and sincerity about her and an ability to voice her inner thoughts without apprehension. It reminded him of how his mother and father would behave towards him and Nicholas, and even still. With a true sense of self and without ego. That was it, there was no ego with Chrissy, and he found that so attractive and magnetic to his soul.

Thomas considered how his whole life had tilted on an axis since last night. How it had taken another road than that he had imagined. He now had a nephew whom he loved more than anything already and a woman whom he very much wanted to keep in his life. He had never wanted this with any other woman; he would always find their company a strain once their desires had been sated. With Chrissy, he felt there was no need to shield himself or be guarded about his thoughts in case she guessed them. He reminded himself that he must, however, tread carefully around her for fear of overwhelming her. For once he looked to the future with optimism.

Nico had told him that Chrissy worked in the cafe below their flat, and he thought that must make life a little easier for taking care of Nico, as he already knew that he had not started nursery yet. He wished Chrissy were in a more financially secure position. He wanted her to have choices in her life, he wanted to take care of her, but felt intuitively that she would want to be independent. He would support her in whatever she decided and he would be her buffer.

It was clear that Chrissy had left Waite and Sons to be Nico's mother when he had been born. Anne had led Chrissy to believe that his

51

family cared little about what became of her pregnancy, when in truth they had no notion of it. Thomas controlled his feelings of anger and was determined to adopt the same of spirit of grace towards Anne that Chrissy fostered. The flat they lived in was in very poor condition and Thomas thought that if Anne really were making any decent money from modelling, Chrissy and Nico were seeing none of it. It worried him that the flat seemed to require some restructuring and decoration, but maybe he would lend support in an appropriate manner that would not hurt Chrissy's pride.

Thomas had taken photos and selfies of them throughout the afternoon, especially for his parents. And, while demolishing his second ice cream of the day, Nico had his first conversation with his grandparents. Thomas and Chrissy watched as the little boy licked his ice cream and then wandered around them like an adult, conversing with his grandparents on the phone. Thomas had spoken to them when Nico said goodbye, and his mother and father had both sounded tearful but so very happy about being able to speak to Nico and the prospect of seeing him soon.

Back in the playground, it was time for Nico's newly conquered slide, which he revelled in as Thomas and Chrissy waited at the bottom to ensure he landed without hurting himself. By the end of his numerous turns on the slide, they were all having a good laugh. The sun was going down and it felt like time had passed so quickly.

'Home time now, Nico,' said Chrissy as Nico slid down again.

'Ah, Mama one more time. No, two more, Mama, pleeeeease!' he begged, as she gave him a firm sideways glance and Thomas pulled a face.

'OK, OK,' she laughed at them. 'Catch me up, make it fast guys,' she flung over her shoulder as they took their positions and she slowly began walking to the exit of the play area. Thomas ran to catch up with her, with Nico sitting on his shoulders and giggling, 'Wooooooow!'

The sight made Chrissy catch her breath. This is what she had wanted for Nico. This was what he was missing. A father figure. It bought a tear to her eye and she quickly looked away to dry her eyes. She didn't want this day to end. Who knew what the future held? Of course, Thomas and his family would be seeing more of Nico once he was used to them, and she wanted just a little more time with Thomas, rather than just at pick-ups and drop-offs. Thomas wondered what had caused Chrissy's change of mood. It was as if she had withdrawn from him and was avoiding his gaze. He strained his neck to catch a better glimpse of her face without unseating Nico from his shoulders, which was next to impossible.

'Do you have to leave early, Tom? We could rustle up some dinner at home if you like,' Chrissy offered, as Nico squealed in agreement.

'That would be lovely, Chrissy, thank you,' Thomas said, as Nico yelped, 'Yes!'

Thomas was very pleased to spend more time with Chrissy and Nico, of course, but wondered if Medusa (aka Anne) would make an appearance. Thomas asked Chrissy whether Anne would be home soon, and Chrissy confirmed that Anne hadn't been back to the flat for a year before the last few Fridays, so answered honestly that she did not have a clue.

The car ride consisted of Thomas explaining to Nico that his grandfather and father all had the same job, which was to make sure that the laws kept working, and that he was a businessman. Nico asked lots of questions and decided that he didn't like the idea of helping criminals and he would rather be a businessman like Uncle Tom. Both Chrissy and Thomas laughed soundly at Nico's rather simplistic logic.

Arriving at the flat, Thomas retrieved Wombie and Nico started watching his favourite hero dogs, while Chrissy put the kettle on for some tea, which, though not a sexy drink, was a favourite of them both. Chrissy gave Nico a glass of strawberry milk, which he loved, while she and Thomas sat in the kitchen to drink their tea.

Thomas looked into his tea and broached the subject. 'Chrissy, my parents would very much love to meet Nico.'

'Of course, they must,' Chrissy agreed. 'Do they want to come here and see him? They can come whenever they want. I think Nico needs to get used to you a little more, after which you can take him to your parents.'

'Would you have any objection to bringing Nico to see them?' asked Thomas.

Chrissy had not imagined that she would have to play any part in the equation. She hesitated. Thomas read the surprise in her eyes. 'Chrissy, in the ways that matter the most, you are Nico's mother and in so being we will always want you in our lives as long as you want to be.'

Once again, Chrissy's eyes misted up. She felt the genuineness at the heart of Thomas's declaration and was touched. 'That is such a lovely thing to say and I welcome it,' she said. 'Well, in that case, how about tomorrow? I can bring him.'

'I was hoping you would say that!' Thomas confirmed happily. 'No need for you to bring him. I will collect you both tomorrow. My parents live in Surrey, as you know, but you may not know I live with them now, and it isn't too far from here. Thank you, Chrissy.' Thomas rubbed his palms on his trouser thighs. Chrissy reached to place a hand over one of his hands.

'Ah, Tom, you don't need to thank me – it's all for Nico, and nothing is too much for him,' Chrissy said.

Thomas covered her hand with his and lifted her hand to his mouth to kiss the knuckle. His lips poised on her skin and remained there as he closed his eyes and then slowly opened them to look into her eyes. Her hand quivered and she drew in a sharp, surprised breath. His eyes spoke of hunger and longing that melted her bones. Nothing else existed except them, and time stood still. He wanted to kiss her. Would she let him? He drew his face closer to hers and his tongue flicked out to gently touch the bow of her lips, and then his lips lay on hers, gently covering them whole and applying a little pressure as they moved sensually against hers. She kissed him back, slowly and reticently. He still held her hand and his other hand cradled her chin and guided her movements to receive his kiss. Then as soon as it had started, he withdrew his mouth. Chrissy felt

54

bereft and couldn't help the look of loss that reflected in her eyes.

'Chrissy, I won't be able to resist you if you look at me like that,' Thomas begged in a ragged voice. 'I have wanted you for a very long time, believe it or not, since you were at Waite's.' He smiled as she looked surprised. 'Yes, even then you were a siren forbidden to me. I didn't want to disturb and complicate your life with the havoc of mine, so I stayed away from you, occasionally sauntering over to the criminal department with no business other than to catch a glimpse of you.'

She looked more surprised than ever. All those times she thought he had been passing and didn't see her. Had it really been that she was all he wanted to see? Chrissy found it hard to believe, but on the other hand, this magnetism they now felt for each other was undeniable.

A sudden crashing sound rung from the lounge and Nico shouted 'Ohhhh!' Chrissy and Thomas both sprung to their feet. Domino ran into the kitchen and hid under the table as Nico chased after her.

'Nico, stop!' Chrissy ordered. Nico did as he was told and Chrissy eyed him for any injury, raising her eyebrows at him.

'Mama, I'm not hurt; I was trying to catch Domino and she ran...' Nico looked at Chrissy, clearly hiding something. Thomas watched amused as she and Nico tiptoed around each other, instinctively knowing what the other had done.

'What did you break, Nico?' Chrissy inquired, knowing that he had in fact broken something. Thomas guessed that this came with years of experience.

'Mama, you didn't like it anyway!' Nico shouted as he ran into the lounge, followed by Chrissy. She looked at the small coffee table, which had a crack in the middle and two broken legs, making it look like it had fallen on its face. Chrissy turned to Thomas and smiled, mouthing to him, 'I really hated that table'.

'Nico...' she started, and Nico came forward and sat on the settee.

'Yes, Mama,' he said.

55

'I want a promise from you, OK, and your Uncle Tom is here to witness it, right?' Chrissy said, as Nico nodded. 'Promise Mama that you will not jump around so carelessly again.'

'I won't jump around carelessly, Mama,' Nico repeated.

Chrissy sat next to Nico, and he jumped onto her lap. 'You know, Nico is very special to Mama and Uncle Tom, and he could get hurt, so it's very important,' she said.

Nico held her face in both of his hands and turned her face to his. 'Mama, but I didn't get hurt, and I jumped really high, Mama, shall I show you?'

He got off her lap, but was soon stopped in his tracks. 'Niiiccooo...' Chrissy said in a warning tone.

'Oh, yes, Mama, I promised,' he said, switching the TV on to his required channel and settling on the settee, while Chrissy and Tom set about clearing up the mess. Chrissy mouthed, 'This is my life' at Thomas, as they exchanged a smile.

Chrissy put her hands together once she and Thomas had cleared up the mess. 'Right, what shall we eat then? I can offer pizza, or shepherd's pie or...'

'Shepherd's pie sounds good,' said Thomas.

'I have to admit that Mo, our chef in the cafe, has shepherd's pie downstairs, which is what it'll be. It's very tasty and we could drum up a salad.' Chrissy beckoned Tom to follow her and told Nico they were popping into the cafe to collect the shepherd's pie, to which he replied, 'OK, Mama.' Nico was not a fussy eater; even though his favourite was pasta, he was generally a content little soul.

Thomas followed Chrissy as she unlocked the door that led to the cafe and wedged in the doorstop so Nico could follow if he decided to. Thomas surveyed the cafe, which was tidy and seemed in good repair, as Chrissy went into the kitchen fridge to retrieve the shepherd's pie and another dish. She mouthed 'blueberry cheesecake' at Thomas as he took the dish from her and they both went back upstairs. Chrissy had suggested that Thomas call his parents to let them know that Nico would be coming to see them tomorrow, which he did.

CHAPTER FIVE

C hrissy had tossed a simple salad and they had all sat in the kitchen eating, laughing and talking about anything and everything, especially their trip to see Nico's grandparents tomorrow. Thomas insisted on washing up as Chrissy dried and put away the dishes. She was an intelligent woman and expressed that she wanted to get back into casework once Nico started nursery but she would have to crunch the numbers before deciding. As she talked, a piece of peeling plaster from the ceiling plopped into the dishwater. Horrified, Chrissy looked at the offending material and up at whence it had come, and then looked at Thomas who couldn't restrain a grin to ease her embarrassment. He looked up at the ceiling and its visible cracks and peeling papers, concern etched on his forehead as his eyebrows knitted together. Chrissy forced a small smile on her face and assured him. 'It's not dangerous – Will, the landlord, is waiting for the works order to come through from the surveyor and a date to start repairs on the flat and cafe, so hopefully all the disrepair will be sorted out soon and we will only have to move out for a couple of months. Will has a flat we can move to temporarily.' Thomas thought about this, and the wheels began to turn in his head; he thought he may have a better plan.

After clearing up the dinner things, Thomas witnessed Nico's bathtime, which included a lot of splashing and an invitation for Chrissy to join him. This made her blush and Thomas's groin ache with desire as he tried to stop imagining a naked and wet Chrissy. Thomas pulled a wriggly Nico out of the bath, wrapping him in his heavily cartooned towel and carrying him into the bedroom that he had entered last night under very different circumstances. It was a little room painted in a light lilac colour with a huge toy chest by a wall and a small window opposite. On the walls were many drawings which at a guess were drawn by Nico and a big poster of a dog in a red uniform clearly from a cartoon. By the bedside stood a lamp and a single photo. It was of Nicholas and Anne. He was laughing at the camera, as was Anne. It must have been taken just before he died. Next to that was a picture of Nicholas alone smiling at the camera. Thomas looked down at Nico as he righted himself after jumping on to the narrow bed that he and Chrissy had been sharing yesterday evening. He was reminded of Chrissy's state of undress in the bed yesterday evening, her long legs bent around Nico's sleeping frame and one hand on Nico's chest.

Thomas was perplexed when Nico directed him to kneel next to him, as Chrissy did likewise. Thomas followed suit as Nico and Chrissy put their hands together in prayer. He couldn't remember the last time he prayed but, to his surprise, Nico began talking in lowered tones. 'Dad, Uncle Tom is here; I know you saw him today and we went to the park and had pasta and a lot of fun. Thank you for sending him to us, I really like him.' And with that, he got to his feet and got under the covers of the quilt while directing Chrissy on which book he would like to have read to him.

Thomas was surprised. That he had not expected. His thoughts were cut short by a boisterous Nico demanding his attention. Thomas's book-reading skills were also put to the test when Nico had insisted that he should read all the characters' voices in different tones for all the animals from the exotic destinations. Chrissy had helped with some of the voices, and he had to admit that they both sounded pretty hideous, so he was relieved when Nico finally fell asleep.

Chrissy had left them to it as the book had progressed further and was sitting in the lounge when Thomas popped his head in and said he would be heading off.

Then he approached her. 'Chrissy...'

Chrissy knew he was choked up by Nico's message to Nicholas, and simply said, 'He needs to remember his father.'

Thomas slid a finger down the side of her cheek and looked into her eyes, trying to fathom how this woman could be so generous of spirit and how her thoughts could remain so focused on what was right. He gently moved towards her and as he did so he manoeuvred her easily towards himself, lowering his head slowly to kiss her on the cheek and then her neck. She sighed and leant the lower half of her body into him. Her hands spread across his chest; the touch was so gentle but its effect was devastating to his composure. Thomas reminded himself that he needed to take this slowly with Chrissy. She was not the normal kind of woman he encountered who knew the rules of the game. This was another game entirely, a game entrenched in reality and a game that he wanted to last forever. He surprised himself as he vowed that nothing but a lifetime with Chrissy would do. He would not rush her. He would build a life with her with stealth, patience, passion and love. She had embarrassed herself, she thought, as he placed distance between them by moving slightly away from her, and she made to move further away, her head bent. He put his hand out and lifted her chin.

'Chrissy,' he said firmly, forcing her to look at him. His eyes were sombre. 'Please don't ever think I don't desire you. I desire you as I have never desired a woman before, but I want to give you time – time to make the right choices for you. I hope you understand?'

'No, I don't, Tom – if we want each other, then what else do we have to decide?'

'Chrissy, this is so hard,' he said, almost begging, and she looked down at his crotch, which clearly showed the battle his mind and body were fighting. She gave it one last attempt as she went to move closer to him, spurred on by the power she felt at being able to weaken his will, and a mischievous smile also appearing as her eyes danced with merriment.

With that, he chuckled and moved away from her and gently let her go. 'Woman, you are the devil. Trust me, Chrissy. It's not very often that I do the right thing. Will you trust me?'

Chrissy nodded. She saw this was important to him, so she became serious, lacing her fingers together to give them something to do other than touch him.

They agreed he would collect them at midday the following day, and Thomas left the flat. He got into the open car door and propelled the window down, waving at Chrissy who still stood at the door. He wished he could have held her tightly against him and ravaged her mouth with his tongue and then rained kisses all over her face. How he would have loved the feel of her skin against his as they shared the passion that burned between them.

His thoughts wandered further back to earlier that evening, and when he had envisioned Chrissy in the bath, wet and sweet-smelling. He would love to join her and smooth the soap down her back. He imagined his hands massaging her shoulders, before sensually circling her waist and resting on her plump breasts. He would gently touch them and then cup them in his hands while he kissed the nape of her neck and her shoulder before returning to gently bite her neck and suck in her flesh. The passion he had for her was powerful. The thoughts of her developed an uncomfortable tightness in his pants, a feeling he was fast becoming familiar with. It was a feeling he was having to endure, just being in the same room with her, and he did not know how long he would be able to resist her.

He composed himself as his parents would be waiting up to hear everything about their Nico. He was right, his mother and father were still awake, and there was no soft glow of light from AJ's apartment, which meant that she was awake and probably waiting with them. He walked into the garden room and was met by three sets of inquiring eyes.

'Hi, guys, I have so much to tell you,' Thomas said as Jo rose from her seat and took his hand, leading him to come and sit with her. It was not unusual for AJ to sit with the family of an evening, although she usually preferred the solitude of her apartment when her working day was done. Thomas ran through the day he had spent with Nico and Chrissy, noting that every minute had been a highlight. It was particularly poignant when Thomas described how Nico had prayed to Nicholas, at which point Jem rose to his feet to study a nearby flower, probably trying to regain his composure.

Jem was the first to speak, as if confirming a theory he had devised. 'Chrissy seems to have bought him up well – from what you say it seems that for all intents and purposes she is Nico's mother, and thus she has a place in our lives.'

At this point Thomas retrieved his phone to show them all pictures from the day. Jem and AJ stood behind the sofa where Thomas and Jo sat to peer at the screen. Jo stopped him at a picture of Nico standing at the top of the slide, she took his phone and peered at it, one hand on her chest and the other holding the phone trembling a little, drinking in every feature of Nico's face. She handed the phone to Jem and reached for his hand. 'He looks just like Nicholas.' There was a contentment in that moment. Then in that quiet room rose an excited discussion about the following day, as AJ held the phone and looked upon little Nico, reeling off delectables that she would prepare for him. A list was quickly made of each of AJ and Thomas's tasks for the visit and they all went to their bedrooms with a bounce in their steps.

Thomas's thoughts again turned back to Chrissy as he got to his room. He opened the door and for the first time saw his room as nothing more than a functional space. It was a large room with a king-size bed and a black dado rail running along the middle of the walls. There was a starkness and emptiness about it. He suddenly longed for softness in the room – a well-worn sofa and a cracked vase with flowers in it; things in his life that had been touched by Chrissy. He became aware of something that had been missing from his adult life and wondered how he had never even known it was missing and how much he needed it. Of course, there had been women in his life, but in comparison to his interaction with Chrissy, his relationships with women had all been very one-dimensional. There would be dinners, maybe theatre or charity events when they had clapped, shared a joke or discussion and then retired to his house in the City for mutual enjoyment. Yes, there had been lust and he had liked these women, but never this depth of caring, when physical contact came second to the natural but profound feeling of peace and rightness that he felt when with Chrissy.

Thomas showered, put on his shorts and slipped into bed. His dreams were of Chrissy who lay with him as they caressed each other slowly and made love until the cracks of dawn peeped through the gaps in the curtain. He smiled as he turned over and sleep took over him.

Chrissy closed the door as Thomas's car drove off. Today had been a lovely day. Nico had been so happy and Thomas had only added to the joy. He had easily slid into the normality of an average day without any awkwardness. It was a different day; she had not felt this complete since her childhood days with Mum and Dad. She was a little apprehensive about tomorrow, but she was also very excited for Nico. He would discover a family who she was sure now would support him throughout his life. She felt very much a third wheel in this dynamic but she could not excuse herself. She had to be there to facilitate and nurture the relationship between Nico and his new-found family. She owed that to Nico and also the memory of Nicholas now that she knew the nature of their feeling for Nico.

Chrissy showered and got into bed and tumbled into a rather disturbed sleep as Nico slumbered carefree next to her. Anne had not returned yet, which was not unusual, but Chrissy had hoped she would be involved in the next stages of Nico meeting his family. Chrissy made a mental note to leave a message for her tomorrow so that she knew where they were. In all honesty, she knew Anne would not be interested in what she and Nico got up to, but she always made sure Anne would know where they were – a sentiment not returned by Anne.

Chrissy and Nico woke early, showered and left the flat early the next morning. Both were clad in jeans, Chrissy in a white T-shirt and Nico in his red Superdog top. They visited the local memorial gardens where there was a bench and plaque in memory of her father and mother, Jay and Kim. Today seemed to be a good day to go. Chrissy had left Anne a note regarding foreseeable plans about awaiting a date for works in the flat and that they would be required to move out into another one of Will's flats in the interim. She also noted their plans for the day and that Thomas was picking them up. She added that she was sorry Anne was not coming with them to Nicholas's parents' home.

Nico was his usual boisterous self as they hopped on to a bus and made the short journey to the gardens. As they arrived at the entrance Nico ran to old Mr Mike and gave him a pound for a water vessel and ran with it to a tap nearby. Chrissy followed Nico as he made the familiar journey to gather the water into the vessel and ran alongside Chrissy with it to the bench. Chrissy had planted a red camellia bush next to the bench when Nico was born, and it had yet to flower. Nico always had the task to water it when they came.

Chrissy sat with Nico and said, 'Why don't you tell Nana and Nani what we did yesterday?' Nico didn't need any more encouragement as he narrated the events of the day before. As he did so Chrissy found herself mentally filling in the gaps in Nico's story. She voiced her happiness that Nico had met Thomas and was going to meet his grandparents, and how she was confident they would love and spoil him. She also dared to mention her liking Thomas and that she would see what happened between them both.

She began to consider that Thomas was right that they should take it slow, if at all, due to the impact it could have on Nico if things didn't work out. With that, Chrissy resolved that maybe her role would just be to help facilitate the relationship between Nico and his new family, and to then bow out. She had to be realistic and acknowledge that Thomas was out of her league entirely. A billionaire with a waitress – that was the stuff of Hollywood movies, not real life. What was she thinking?

Would she lose Nico? No! She banished that thought. Nico was everything. Chrissy stopped her thoughts running along this negative path. Nico was the most important consideration and she would not think of anything negative about the future. Everything would work out fine, she knew it. Nico ran for more water and came back to pour more into the camellia and they both whispered 'love you' to the spirit of Jay and Kim before returning home. On the bus ride, Chrissy told Nico about Mr Waite and his wife who were his grandparents, and how sad they had been since his dad had gone to heaven. They were looking forward so much to seeing him and he must be kind and gentle to them and give them lots of hugs. Nico acknowledged this as, of course, he was an expert in hugs, wasn't he? 'Yes,' Chrissy agreed, hugging him while he giggled.

Ryan had just parked the car outside Chrissy's flat and got out to open Thomas's door when Nico ran towards Ryan and shook his hand in greeting. Ryan ruffled Nico's hair as Thomas got out of the car, and Nico launched himself at Thomas, who swung him into the air and gave him a great big bear hug. 'Uncle Tom, you're squeezing me,' he giggled. Thomas was surprised to see them out. They seemed to have arrived back from somewhere. Thomas looked for Chrissy, who had just them caught up and was looking incredibly sexy in her denim outfit, fitted short jeans jacket, and a tight-fitting white T-shirt. The T-shirt clung to the outline of her breasts and the short jacket emphasised her small waist.

'We've been to see Nani and Nana; we went on a bus,' Chrissy explained.

'It's my parents' memorial – Nico likes to water his camellia too.'

'The flowers are as old as I am but there have never been flowers on them. Mama says we have to be patient and when the flowers come, they will be red – I love red, Uncle Tom,' Nico gushed, running out of breath. By this time Thomas had set Nico on his feet and Nico had twined his fingers into Thomas's and was pulling him towards the flat.

'Come on in, Tom, we'll just freshen up and we can be on our way,' Chrissy said, leading the way.

'You know where things are – are you OK to fix yourself something to drink while I sort us out?' Chrissy said as they entered the flat, leading a reluctant Nico away.

'Of course, you go ahead,' said Thomas, going into the kitchen and fixing himself and Nico a glass of cold cordial and Chrissy a cup of tea. Nico led him into the lounge, reintroducing him to his friends of the cloth and feline variety. Anne did not seem to have returned.

Chrissy quickly washed her face and applied some face cream and light lipstick, looking at herself in the mirror. She would never be a beauty but she had to admit she had striking features – full lips, and what someone had once called bedroom eyes. Chrissy chuckled as she called Nico to the bathroom to wash his face. She also packed an extra set of clothes and his pyjamas. As with most kids, he often got his clothes dirty. She wasn't sure how late they would be but she took his pyjamas to change him into for when he started to wane, so that she did not have to struggle with his sleeping frame when they got home.

They were ready to go now. Thomas was washing his and Nico's glasses as she entered the kitchen, as if he always did this, and Chrissy did not comment. 'Are we ready?' he asked, looking at her and ruffling Nico's hair. 'Yesss,' Nico said as Chrissy opened the door and they all walked out.

The journey to his parents' home was interrupted by a stop at a DIY outlet. 'Chrissy, you don't mind if we stop here, do you? I thought we could pick up a few things for Nico for Mum and Dad's place. There have been no children in the house since Nicholas was born. It's a pretty new sensation and of course you can take the things home as well?'

'Of course,' she replied, and Nico whooped in excitement.

After an hour Thomas and Nico had loaded the trolley with lots of devices and would have loaded on many more before Chrissy had to intervene. With some reasoning she made Nico choose only two things, namely a skittle set and huge trampoline. Thomas argued that the colouring pencils and books didn't count, so she let him have them too. Thomas watched as Chrissy spoke to Nico about not being too greedy and that he had to pick the two things he really wanted. Thomas would have happily bought Nico the whole store, but also appreciated the need to bring up children with an eye to moderation and restraint.

As Thomas paid for the items, Chrissy and Nico held back and were viewing some plants at the till points. Nico nodded as Chrissy picked out a jasmine plant with little flowers. She told Thomas that she and Nico would like to buy this for Nico's grandma. Thomas smiled and allowed Chrissy to pay for the plant.

The remainder of the journey was spent with Nico excitedly telling Thomas about his starting nursery in January and the fun he had at One O'clock Club in the park with Chrissy. The car slowed as it turned into the short drive leading to Thomas's parents' home. The drive was bordered with red and yellow roses like a floral welcome to guests. The house was huge, with window boxes planted with various flowers and a red flower vale growing on the walls, giving the house a hacienda-type feel. Chrissy could not believe how beautiful this house was. House, she thought, correcting herself – this was not a house, this was a mansion. The view took her breath away. As they approached, she could see that beyond the front door was a rising glass structure like a dome shape and she thought she could see palms brushing the glass. Of course, she must be mistaken, she thought.

Three people were waiting outside the house. Mr and Mrs Waite,

Chrissy recognised, though they seemed to have aged a lot more in the five years since she had last seen them. Also present was a lady about Thomas's mother's age – Chrissy didn't know who she could be. 'There's Mum and Dad and also AJ,' Thomas whispered to Chrissy as she got out of the car. 'AJ is the housekeeper but more a family friend; she helped raise Nicholas and me.'

Nico jumped out of the car as Chrissy reached back in for the jasmine plant they had bought for Thomas's mother. Chrissy called Nico to her and handed it to him, instructing him to give it to his grandma. Thomas waited for her and when she joined him, he placed a supporting hand to the small of her back in encouragement to walk forward with him behind Nico.

Nico walked towards his grandfather, pulled at his sleeve and asked, 'Are you my grandpa?'

Mr Waite turned to Nico, lifted his trouser legs a little and went down on one knee to meet his gaze. 'Yes, my darling,' he said, his voice breaking a little. He reached for Jo's hand and she came forward, similarly going down on to one knee.

'This is your grandma, Nico.' Nico searched her kind eyes and they both took him into their embrace and breathed in the scent of him as their eyes met above his little head. As with all grandparents, they would never have enough of him. Nico handed Jo the jasmine plant and said it was a gift from him and his mama, and they graciously accepted it, commenting on the beautiful scent of the flowers.

Tom finally broke his parents' enchantment. 'Just before we all go inside, Nico, I want you to meet AJ – she helped to raise your daddy Nicholas and me, and she used to make special treats for us.'

AJ came forward and moved her hand towards Nico to offer a handshake, but Nico pulled her hand down to hug her as she bent down to meet it. She chuckled. 'I will be making you treats too, Nico.'

Walking towards Mr Waite, Thomas said, 'Dad, you remember Chrissy?'

'Oh yes, my dear, you are looking well.' Mr Waite smiled at her and turned to his wife. 'And this is my wife, Jo.'

Jo came towards Chrissy, Nico's hands in hers for a moment, and then kissed her and gave her a big hug. 'Call us Jem and Jo,' she said, and AJ embraced her too, welcoming her with a warm smile.

CHAPTER SIX

*C*J led the way into the house, followed by Thomas and Chrissy. Nico held back, putting each of his hands into his grandparents' hands.

Chrissy was taken aback as she entered the hallway of the house, which sprung into what she could only describe as the largest conservatory she had ever seen outside Kew Gardens. As soon as she entered, she felt a warm air that seemed to be circulating around the enormous foyer. The foyer was constructed almost entirely of glass and all the walls were mostly covered by huge palms and many varieties of flowers, the scents of which Chrissy felt she could bask in forever. There was also the relaxing sound of trickling water somewhere – it was a veritable feast for the senses. Thomas watched as Chrissy entered the house. She was as enthralled by it, as he had hoped, and Nico released his grandparents' hands and ran further into the foyer to gaze at all the plants and flowers.

The foyer was far too big to be crowded and various little paths led away from the central walkway. Jem and Jo smiled as Jem said, 'I see you are taken with the foyer, Chrissy.' She nodded, delight shining in her eyes. 'Well, this was all Jo – she had a vision in mind that we absolutely loved and which Tom made real, and there's more too,' Jem promised as they walked through the foyer along a path and finally came to a large seating area, with three couches making a circle and various little tables and flora overhanging. It was decorated in apricot and silver with a glass coffee table in the middle. There was also a sewing box that had knitting needles and a work in progress laid on top. 'So, here is the garden room, where you will usually find Jem and I,' Jo said as she invited Chrissy to sit down.

Chrissy noticed that some of what appeared to be glass panels were actually mirrors and that there were family photos scattered around the various arrangements, particularly where they were seated now.

Nico sat in between his grandparents. Thomas and Chrissy sat on another sofa as Nico explained the people in his life, including Mama, Mum (Thomas mouthed Anne's name as his parents looked up at him, confused), Mo, Sandy and Uncle Will, not forgetting Wombie and Domino. His grandparents hung on every word that Nico said, thirsty to drink in five missed years of his life.

AJ soon excused herself as she had some tarts in the oven that she had to attend to. Nico's hyper-attentive ears heard that, of course. 'I love jam tarts, AJ, are they strawberry ones?' he asked excitedly.

'Well, as it happens, they may well be,' AJ smiled.

Nico rose from his seat as if to go to inspect, looking at Chrissy for permission. 'Of course, go, if AJ doesn't mind, darling' she said as Nico ran to take AJ's hand and be led into the kitchen.

'You have a lovely home, Mrs Waite,' began Chrissy.

'Now, that will all stop right now,' said Mr Waite. 'You will call us Jem and Jo.'

'Yes, yes,' said Chrissy.

'We cannot tell you how much it means to us to find out about Nico, and we are indebted to you for raising him so well,' said Jem, and then he hesitated, before adding, 'We do not want to interfere with your upbringing of him but ask only that you let us play a part in his life, and let us ease your path so that you can concentrate on him without any hindrance or impediments.'

'Will you let us do that, Chrissy?' Jo asked apprehensively, her fingers twisting in her lap.

Chrissy's heart went out to them both as Thomas bent to look at them too, knowing it must be hard to see his parents so vulnerable. This family was seeking her permission when they could have come in all heavy-handed and demanded. Chrissy was humbled and decided to put her cards on the table. 'Look, Jo, Jem and Tom, the loss of Nicholas was devastating for you all and I appreciate the existence of Nico would be like a lifeline to you. He is my lifeline too, but more than that, I want what is best for him – and what is best for him is to have as many people in his life that love him as possible. I do not feel threatened in any way by your wish to have him in your lives. I welcome this. We will find a way that works and we will all work to make Nico the very best of young men.'

Chrissy felt that she had clearly expressed her true feelings, and could almost feel the relief of all the others in the room. Thomas did not believe he could think any more highly of Chrissy than he already did, but she always seemed to surpass his expectations. Her presence seemed to fill a place with peace. There then followed discussions about Chrissy's work and Anne's noticeable lack of involvement in the lives of Chrissy and Nico. Chrissy spoke lovingly about the home she and Nico shared, though admitting it needed some work, which would be starting soon.

'Oh, you must come and stay with us until the works are completed, Chrissy,' Jo interjected. 'We insist'.

Had he not been seated, Thomas felt confident that he would have fallen over. Good work, mother, he silently rejoiced. She had material-ised plans that he had yet to formulate. Yes, she could stay here and he could see her every day, if not several times a day, he thought, using every ounce of willpower to avoid rubbing his hands with glee.

'No, Jo it wouldn't work,' said Chrissy, but Jo would brook no argument.

'Oh we will make it work,' she said, and then added, with some reluctance, Chrissy thought, 'and of course Anne is also welcome.'

It felt like it was decided, Chrissy thought to herself, but how could this work? 'Let's see how it pans out,' she said in a conciliatory tone.

Jo realised that she was being a little heavy-handed and carefully said, 'Of course, if it is workable, Nico can have his own room when you come to stay and there are many other guest rooms – that's if it works for everybody...' she trailed off. It would be a great way for Nico to get to know Nicholas's family, Chrissy thought, and the cafe was going to be closed anyway. She couldn't think of an argument against it.

Nico entered the lounge carrying a plate with two tarts on it, while AJ carried the remainder on a large plate. He gently placed his plate on the coffee table and excitedly ran to Chrissy, crashing into her knees and then climbing on to her lap. 'Mama, I tried an apricot tart and it was yummier than the strawberry one!' he said.

'That's lovely, darling,' said Chrissy, running her fingers through his curly hair. He was soon going to outgrow her lap, she thought.

'Come her, Nico,' Thomas called to him. 'Shall we show Grandma and Grandpa what we bought today?'

'Oh yes!' Nico's eyes lit up as he ran to take Thomas's outstretched hand, chatting about going into the garden as they left to get the things from the car.

Jo approached Chrissy as Jem got up. 'Come, Chrissy let's go into the garden'. Jem led them through another path that led to the side of the garden and walked around to the back patio.

AJ set the tarts on to the garden table as they all sat on the patio. It was a huge garden that extended as far as the eye could see, with a lush green lawn and various border plants and, set back further, a few pink magnolia and rhododendron trees and an area with only rose bushes. As Chrissy looked on, she could make out a tennis court and a large outbuilding and what looked like a little path that ran along the far side of the garden. Jem's eyes followed hers and he informed her, 'That's my potting shed and that trail leads to an allotment and greenhouse. I enjoy pottering around in my garden and spend a lot of time out there now that I'm retired. The senior partner now runs the firm. It would have been Nicholas, had he been alive today...' he trailed off into thoughts of what could or should have been. Jo put a hand on Jem's arms and her eyes comforted him as he sat down. AJ returned with a pot of tea and a jug of cordial with glasses.

'Now, will we be having lunch out here or inside?' AJ asked, and after a short discussion among the group it was decided to have it outside. AJ had prepared a platter of cold meats, focaccia, a pasta dish and salad for them all and sat with them as they waited for Nico and Thomas.

'You know, the criminal department has been quite unstable since you left, so many different solicitors coming and going,' Jem told Chrissy. 'We are currently without a manager. Such a pitiful state.' He looked beneath hooded eyes at Chrissy for a reaction. 'We really could do with you back with us, you know, dear, and we are also merging with Cartwright and Sons, which means an even larger criminal department. So many jobs are at stake...' He watched Chrissy, but there was no reaction.

Jo drew in an outraged breath. 'Jem! Chrissy is a guest in this house and you accost her with this! This is really not on. I know you worry about the firm and its future, but Chrissy must have enough on her plate.'

'Yes, yes of course, I'm sorry.'

'That's not a problem, Jem, I understand how hard it is to find staff for criminal cases, let alone those that may be legally aided,' Chrissy sympathised, knowing that criminal departments were struggling nationwide. What Jem had said tempted her, and she would think about it in private.

At this point Nico and Thomas entered the garden through a side gate, Nico carrying the skittle set with difficulty and Jesse and Thomas carrying the trampoline. 'We are just going to assemble the trampoline,' Thomas shouted as he walked to the potting shed for some tools, followed by Nico.

'Get your tools, but let's eat before you start,' Jo shouted, to which

Thomas raised an arm in agreement. AJ started dishing out the food on plates and consulted Chrissy on what Nico would have, as Thomas and Nico re-emerged with a tool set.

Jem and Jo were sitting next to Chrissy. Jesse had unpacked some of the trampoline parts as Nico and Thomas deposited the tool set by the trampoline on the lawn. All three of them then raced to the table, both men allowing Nico to win. Nico ran to Chrissy, gasping as he climbed on to the seat next to her. Thomas sat next to Nico and rasped, 'Wow, Nico, you are so fast!'

'Yes, Uncle Tom, I can be there on the double,' said Nico, mimicking his favourite doggy hero. Everybody at the table laughed.

'So, Nico what are you going to eat?' asked Jo, coming around to Nico's seat. 'AJ has made pasta – we heard you love pasta.'

'Yes, please,' Nico said as Chrissy rose to her feet.

'Nico, why don't you sit in Grandma's chair and you sit in mine so you can sit between Grandma and Grandpa. Wouldn't that be nice, Nico?' Chrissy made eye contact with Nico, who immediately nodded enthusiastically as he recognised this was the kindness he and Chrissy had spoken about earlier. Jo thanked Chrissy, touched at this invitation, and exchanged a happy glance with Jem. Thomas pulled out the chair on his other side and was able to concentrate solely on Chrissy as the other four adults indulged the table's favourite person.

Chrissy sat down next to Thomas. 'So, I hear that there are problems with the criminal department at Waite's,' she said.

'Yes, and we're trying to avoid closing it down. We just can't get someone to head it. Also, with the merger with old man Cartwright's firm, I'm afraid one of the casualties may be redundancies all around.'

Chrissy knew that criminal firms were a desert to recruitment. 'I must say I loved the work,' she said, almost nostalgically.

'Any chance I could tempt you back, even temporarily?' asked Thomas.

'It's not the right time – I have the cafe to run, but then there is also

Nico to take care of and my situation at present allows me to do both,' Chrissy said.

Not being one to pass up an opportunity, Thomas jumped at an idea. 'Well, you admitted that you would be having to temporarily move to another place and the cafe would be closed too when renovations begin,' he said.

Chrissy had thought of this as well, and he was right. Could now possibly be a time when she could switch careers? No, of course not – there was still Nico's care, which was a priority.

Thomas picked up on the silent thoughts running through her mind. He could tell she was attracted to going back to the law and he so wanted her back too. He could have her close to him. The thought warmed him. 'Just promise me you won't dismiss it and I don't want to scare you off, but if we are thinking this could happen then I have a way.' He decided to put his thoughts into words in front of everyone before he had time to think about how pie-in-the-sky it may sound. 'Listen, guys.' Everybody looked at him. 'I know Chrissy would like to go back to her career in law, specifically criminal law, and we also have to factor in that taking care of Nico is a priority.'

'I can take care of myself, Uncle Tom, I can, Grandpa,' Nico piped up, and all around the table smiled.

'I know you can, buddy, but let's make your mama happy,' continued Thomas, sending Nico a conspiratorial wink, and Nico blinked in agreement, making all the adults laugh. 'So, with the construction work about to take place at Chrissy's flat and the fact that she may not be working at the cafe in that time I have an ideal solution for a temporary basis, but if it works then it could be a long-term plan.' He stopped.

'Well, what is it, Tom?' Jem burst out after a silence. Although it was all worked out in his head, Thomas had omitted the explanation to his avid audience.

'Oh yes, so Nico will be taken care of and will get to know us all, *and*

Chrissy can come work for the firm again by moving in here with us!'

Chrissy looked on open-mouthed, while Jo clapped her hands together and squeezed her eyes shut for a moment. All those around the table were silent while calculating the merit of the idea, and it was foolproof. All eyes looked at Chrissy, including Nico, who had got off his seat and was jumping up and down next to his grandparents.

'This is so very kind of you all,' said Chrissy, 'but so much needs to be worked out before such a decision can take place, and then there is Anne and Will.'

'Of course,' Thomas said solemnly, unable to believe that this could be a perfect plan, the voicing of which may bring it into being.

AJ interrupted the calculations going on in everybody's heads. 'Let's eat now, shall we? Then we have jam tarts, fruit and cream.'

'Yum!' said Nico.

They ate while conversing easily. Nico entertained them with stories of his wonder dogs while he devoured the pasta, and then started on his dessert, upon which Jem was pouring copious amounts of fresh cream. 'Uncle Tom, will we go to build the trampoline soon? Jesse and I can help you as we are the able-bodied men in the house,' said Nico, leaving everybody in peals of laughter, which went over his head. Chrissy had recently been explaining disabled signs to him and she often referred to him as the man of the house, and so Nico had taken the mantle and run amok with it, it seemed.

'Yes, of course, Nico, but let me see your muscles then, young man,' Thomas joined in.

Nico lifted his arm and showed the table, turning to Jem and saying 'Look, Grandpa, feel them. I'm strong, aren't I?'

'Oh, yes, Nico, they're pretty impressive,' Jem said, feeling the softness of his upper arm and then turning to Thomas. 'Tom, you've got your man here.'

While the other adults chatted, the three able-bodied men of the house

77

went to build a trampoline. AJ and Chrissy then cleared away the lunch dishes and stacked the dishwasher together. AJ confirmed that she had been with the family since the birth of Nicholas and that she lived in a self-contained flat in the main house. Although it was just her at weekends, during the week she had cleaners in every day and someone to help in the kitchen.

Jo and AJ embarked with Chrissy on a tour of the huge house. The stairs from the kitchen came to a split, leading to the left and right wings of the house. Anne's quarters were to the left of the right staircase, after which there was the further wing of guest rooms, and the family's bedrooms were to the right of AJ's apartment, where there were also guest bedrooms. They passed Nicholas's room, which was sparsely decorated; it seemed untouched and clearly unlived in for some time. Jo admitted that they couldn't do anything with it and besides they did not need the room for any other purpose.

Jem and Jo's room was decorated in paisley set in light greens and pink with pine furniture and flowery paintings. It was a warm and cosy room. The landing had small side tables at intervals that had either small Grecian sculptures on them or flower vases, and the walls were adorned with various paintings of woodlands, flowers and seascapes. The guest rooms were tastefully decorated in pink or blues and whites with double beds. Thomas's room was at the end of the corridor. It was large, decorated with a single black line running along the walls and black fitted cupboards. An abstract black and white painting hung on one wall. Nothing was out of place and it seemed a very impersonal room. All the rooms had en suite bathrooms. It really was a beautiful house.

They descended the stairs and turning back on themselves to the right there were various rooms including a library with wall-to-wall bookshelves stacked with books and two large desks side by side in front of huge glass doors. Two chesterfields were facing each other with a coffee table in the middle and the smell of leather was prominent in the room. There were two lounges that they just called the silver room and the blue room. The silver room contained glitzy furnishings, chrome fittings and silver-framed mirrors, while the blue room was decorated in dark and royal blues with velveteen furniture and curtains. It was a lush-looking room that Chrissy instantly fell in love with. 'We love this room too,' said Jo. Every part of it was designed to cushion the occupier in its opulence, from the big dragon-shaped chandelier dangling from a high ceiling to the two seating areas, both with soft deep-blue furnishings. There was also a games room in a retro diner style with red and white leather seating, with a huge TV, a snooker table and a television, and along the wall was a big open cupboard stocked with games such as Monopoly and puzzles and other gadgets.

As they walked back towards the main staircase, they turned back on themselves again, this time to the left, and Chrissy recognised the path to the garden room. As one went further into the house there was a door to a small sewing room with a sewing machine and soft flowery furniture. Next to this was the large kitchen in hues of peach and grey. The kitchen had a door leading to the garden and another two small doors, the first leading to a large larder and the other door leading into a utility room with a counter space and a door leading to the garden.

Opposite the kitchen and under the main staircase was another door. It seemed that this house had so many surprises, as this door led to a leisure facility that held a large heated swimming pool, and to the left of the pool was a table and a door leading into the garden. To the right of it was a wall and behind the wall were four doors. Two in the middle led to a steam room and a sauna, while to the far right was a ladies' changing room and men's changing room. Both had various floats and swimming attire neatly folded on to a few open shelves.

There were also two Jacuzzis, one that led straight from the pool and another sunken one set apart from it in a little alcove with dimmed lighting. As Chrissy looked at the sunken Jacuzzi, Nico came running in from the garden, with Thomas close behind him.

'Mama, Mama, come on, we've built the tramp...' Nico trailed off as he saw the swimming pool, his eyes the size of saucers. 'Wow, Mama, a swimming pool! Can we go for a swim, Uncle Tom?'

Thomas chuckled and ruffled Nico's hair. 'Of course, buddy, but do you want to have a go on the trampoline first?'

Nico was obviously conflicted, but then decided it would be the trampoline first and then the swim.

'I don't think we will have any trunks in Nico's size,' Thomas said aloud.

Chrissy said that he had a spare pair of pants in his bag so he could just get in with those on, which everybody agreed was a good idea. Thomas agreed to bring Nico's bag in from the car before the swim.

'You could join us for a swim – I'm sure you'll find something to fit in the ladies' changing room,' Thomas said, not being able to resist his gaze drifting slowly up her body and resting on her face, which was aflame.

AJ grinned, but neither of them noticed, as nobody was watching her. 'Now what have we here,' AJ thought, her mind already racing with new-found hopes.

Uncle and nephew left the pool room, followed by AJ and Chrissy who joined Jem and Jo in the garden room. It was quite a big trampoline with a safety net around it and Thomas stood holding the flap open as Nico bounded through it and started to jump. Thomas pulled up the zip to secure the net as Nico bounced to his heart's content, squealing in delight.

'You are staying for the day, aren't you, Chrissy?' asked Jo.

'Oh yes, especially now Nico has pretty much decided that he will be swimming later on,' replied Chrissy.

'Chrissy,' Jo began hesitantly, 'how do you come to be ferrying Nico around rather than Anne, and, well, he calls you Mama.'

This was a rather loaded question and Chrissy believed in being honest in these awkward situations. She explained that Anne had a career to think about and they had both agreed that Chrissy would be the primary caregiver while Anne concentrated on her modelling. It worked very well and Nico called Anne 'Mum'. He certainly had the capacity to accept this while understanding the importance of both their roles in life.

Thomas was instructing Nico on the trampoline as an elderly man entered the garden from the side walkway. He was accompanied by a young boy around Nico's age. Jem rose from his seat upon seeing him and walked towards him.

'I thought I heard a child laughing,' the man said to Thomas, as the young boy with him ran towards the trampoline, grasping the mesh.

Thomas shook the man's hand. 'Hello, Jon and Jamie,' he said to the man and the boy with him, as Jem patted the man on the back and ruffled the young boy's hair. Thomas walked back to the trampoline and was conversing with Jamie, which appeared to be the little boy's name. Tom lifted Jamie and opened the zip of the trampoline, handing Jamie on to the bouncy bed. Thomas leaned in to speak to Nico, as Nico sat next to Jamie and put a welcoming arm around Jamie's shoulder. Both boys talked for a few moments and then began jumping on the trampoline, laughing and falling about. Jo explained to Chrissy that Jon was their neighbour and Jamie was his four-year-old grandson.

Jem walked back to the ladies sitting in the conservatory and made introductions between Jon and Chrissy. Jem glowed with pride as he confirmed that Nico was Nicholas's son, his grandson. Jon congratulated Jo and Jem on being united with Nico, and there began an easy conversation on the joys and tribulations of being a grandparent. Jon was a widower whose son James and daughter-in-law Erica had moved in with him while they were building their own house nearby. They would often come over and sit with the Waites, and little Jamie loved the swimming pool and splashing around when the adults ventured in with him. Jamie seemed to be Jon's constant companion of late.

AJ started to clear away the lunch items and Chrissy assisted her in making pleasant conversation. Jo asked them to work out what should be on the dinner menu as Chrissy could tell AJ what she and Nico liked and disliked. Chrissy and AJ decided that a lasagne, fresh dinner rolls and salad would be nice with an apple crumble and custard. Chrissy said she would love to be able to make the lasagne and apple crumble, but AJ flatly refused, as Chrissy was a guest. As Chrissy and AJ cleared away the remainder of the debris, Chrissy said, addressing Jo and Jem as well as AJ, 'I would feel much more at home if I could truly contribute to the day and, besides, I do love to cook.'

Jo threw her hands up and said, 'It looks like a done deal, then.'

AJ and Chrissy had just sat down as Nico and Jamie came running into the garden room, followed by Thomas, who sat down next to Chrissy again. He drew his head nearer to her as Nico and Jamie enthused about the fun they were having. 'How are you doing?' Thomas whispered.

Chrissy turned to him and laid her hand on his. 'I'm enjoying myself; you have a lovely home and family. Nico is in his element, as you can see.'

'Yes, he's very energetic and with Jamie, they are a force to be reckoned with,' agreed Thomas.

Thomas had set up the skittle set for the boys to play and they were doing very well resetting the game and ensuring that they didn't throw the ball too hard. Chrissy got up and started to pour AJ's homemade lemonade for those at the table and called to Nico and Jamie to come and have some of it too. Both boys ran to Chrissy as Nico introduced his new friend to her.

'Mama, this is Jamie – he lives next door – and Jamie, this is my Mama; I have two mamas. My other mum is not here.' Jamie swallowed the lemonade as he nodded at Nico.

'It's good to meet you, Jamie, I'm Chrissy,' she said, once Jamie had finished his drink, and he gave her a winning smile.

'Nico's mama' said Jamie.

'Yes, Jamie, and call me Chrissy,' she said, her heart melting at how sweet he was.

'We sometimes go for a swim in the pool here – do you think Nico and I could go swimming today?'

'I don't see why not Jamie,' said Chrissy.

The other adults at the table smiled as this dialogue between the two.

'Grandma,' said Nico, 'Can Jamie and his grandpa stay for dinner?'

'Why ever not?' replied Jo, delighted at the suggestion, and looked to Jon for consent.

'Well, that's decided, then – we will call Erica and let her know not to hold dinner for us,' Jon said.

Both Nico and Jamie whooped and ran back to their game of skittles.

'So, what do you like to do for fun, Chrissy?' Thomas asked.

'Well, everything kind of revolves around Nico, really, but we like galleries, the cinema and visiting historical places. I haven't been to the theatre for a while, it's terribly expensive, and Mr Fidget here probably wouldn't be able to sit through a whole production, anyway,' Chrissy said, nodding her head towards Nico. 'I also like reading usually fiction and am fascinated by Tudor history. I have fond memories of holidays to Cornwall with my parents. They were some of the best times of my life.'

She sat back, and suddenly realised that she had shared more than was required of her, and that she had got a little carried away. It was not very often that she was asked that question and never recently by a man. Sandy always said she gave off a 'don't come near me' vibe, and so no man dared get into her airspace.

'Sorry, I went off on one,' said Chrissy.

'Don't be, I want to know more, which is why I asked,' said Thomas, though it seemed like his thoughts were somewhere else. He sat back in his chair; it was at an angle to Chrissy's, which gave him a full view of her face. When talking about her likes he felt her relax further and he felt almost transported with her to her favourite places.

'My maternal grandfather used to holiday with his parents in Cornwall and he loved to travel there with my mother, father, Anne and I. We would take the car and load up all our luggage for the trip of some eight hours. We would take a Thermos of tea and sandwiches and stop on the way for breakfast as we would be on the road from four in the morning. I loved our journey there and passing Stonehenge. Then there was the 'nearly there' group of trees which heralded just that.'

Chrissy gave a teary smile at Thomas and quickly looked away. He wondered how someone could open themselves up so fully as Chrissy did. There was a vulnerability about her that she wasn't afraid to show, which in another way was also a strength. It made Thomas want to protect her against the cruel hands of time and other people who would prey on such a tender heart.

'Well, as it's a family tradition, maybe we can continue it,' Thomas said, his kindness making Chrissy smile. They both looked over to Jamie and Nico as both boys lay on their backs under a tree, seemingly studying something of interest and having a quiet discussion.

'Maybe it's time for that swim,' Thomas said to Chrissy, and inviting everybody else to join in. Jem and Jon said they would rather not and would play cards in the swimming lounge. AJ and Jo were game, so everyone made to leave the table and head to the swimming pool, calling to Nico and Jamie to come, at which they bolted ahead of the adults excitedly.

CHAPTER SEVEN

*A*J and Jo led Chrissy to the female changing room and Thomas took the boys to the male changing section. AJ presented Chrissy with a black one-piece bathing suit that had a square neck and straps and was decent save for the devilishly low-cut back. But it was by far the most modest swimming costume in the cupboard, so Chrissy donned it. AJ and Jo changed too and led the way out to the pool. It was a heated room and pool but Chrissy still felt a shiver, mainly because she was painfully aware of how much of her back she was revealing. She could hear Nico and Jamie screeching in the pool as Thomas laughed. Nico had learned to swim when he was just two. It was one of the things Chrissy had insisted on, and it seemed Jamie could also swim. As she approached, Nico cannonballed into the pool, followed by Jamie. Both boys were clearly daredevils. Jo and AJ had already walked into the middle of the pool and were sitting in the adjoining Jacuzzi, talking. Nico and Jamie were now swimming under each other's legs near AJ and Jo, who was now keeping an eye on them, and Jem and Jon had settled to play cards.

Thomas was surprised by Jamie and Nico catapulting themselves into the pool and amazed at how both boys had gone straight into a confident swim. As the splashes subsided, his eye was caught by slow movement at

85

the other end of the pool. Chrissy had emerged from the ladies' changing area. She was wearing a black one-piece swimming costume which, though it sufficiently covered her curves, actually accentuated them and clung to every contour of her body. This was a treat, Thomas thought. Her back was exposed right down to her hips, and the sight of two partial dimples on her lower back made his pulse begin to race as he noticed how gracefully she swayed as she walked. He drank in the sight of her as her hips were submerged into the water, and he was grateful for that very water, which hid the extent of his arousal at seeing her. The sound of Nico and Jamie easily reduced his arousal to parental guidance as he swam towards Chrissy. He stood in the water as it came to his waist now and he held his hand out to Chrissy, who took it. As she became submerged, he seemed to hesitate. Chrissy felt shy as she felt rather than saw Thomas's smouldering look at her. She felt naked and all she could think of was his muscular hairy chest, arms and chiselled stomach.

He reached her and she began to chatter nervously. 'It's been so long since I've been able to just swim. I'm always wary to keep an eye on Nico, so this it will be nice...'

With a grin, Thomas challenged her. 'OK, then, let's do a few lengths, shall we? See if you've still got it.'

Both he and Chrissy struck out into the water towards the deep end. They swam for several lengths before Chrissy breathlessly stopped and a cheer went up around the pool. Both Nico and Jamie cheered the loudest, shouting, 'Woo, that was good!'

Chrissy stood with both hands on her hips, the water coming to her waist, and laughed, speaking quickly between grasped breaths. 'Look at me, I'm so rusty and unfit.'

Thomas couldn't look away from her and whispered as he approached her. 'Yes, let's look at you – you're the least rusty thing I've ever seen.' He swam under the water, brushing his body against her thighs, and came to stand right behind her, surprising her, and then she quickly stepped away, her heart beating fast. AJ watched as Thomas's glance met hers and a smile passed between them.

They completed several more lengths companionably and stopped for a breather, before sitting in the Jacuzzi for a while with AJ and Jo and joining in with the discussion on whether it would be a good idea to trail a wisteria along the front of the house, which Chrissy wholeheartedly agreed with. AJ and Jo then went into the steam room, leaving Thomas and Chrissy in the Jacuzzi.

Chrissy felt the heat immediately increase tenfold as she realised she was alone with Thomas at close proximity. The warmth of the bubbles and the gentle pressure around her body from the jets added to the turbulence of her emotions. She felt an undeniable attraction to Thomas. He said he was attracted to her too yesterday, but had halted her. Maybe it was because he was so different from her and totally out of her league. They came from different worlds. His was a luxury existence with chauffeurs and mansions for homes, and she was merely eking out a living. Then it suddenly became clear.

She couldn't believe how stupid she had been. She had the answer. He was attracted to her, but it was a passing fancy and purely sexual. Of course he was not looking to have her in his life long term. That would perfectly explain it. Chrissy could not deny the strong attraction she felt for him, and this would probably be the only chance she would have to experience such a passion. She knew then that she loved him and she would enjoy whatever role he gave her, for however a short time it lasted.

Thomas watched as numerous expressions seemed to float across Chrissy's face as she sat so very close to him. He was overcome by how irresistible she was to him. He had to touch her. He moved closer to her and touched her hand under the water. 'Chrissy...'

'Hmm...' she responded, not quite being able to make eye contact with him but jumping a little when she felt his hand on hers. 'You're a simpleton!' she chided herself.

87

'Chrissy, I'm sorry to be so forthright but am I wrong in sensing that there is something between us?' Thomas said, turning his head to look at her.

Chrissy raised her head and looked into his eyes. He was looking intently at her and he could feel something, but he needed to know how she felt too, as he did not think he could keep his attraction bound in, just wanting, without any release. Her eyes were like dark glistening pools with a hidden depth that read of apprehension, and her long eyelashes clung together to frame them beautifully. He was afraid he may have made a grave error. 'I'm sorry, I totally misread the situation.'

Alarmed further, Chrissy knew she had to say something. 'No, Tom,' she whispered. 'No, you didn't misread it. I feel something too. I am attracted to you.' She lowered her eyes. There – she had said it now. Thomas grinned like a Cheshire cat, which was rather funny, and Chrissy burst out laughing, drawing Nico and Jamie's attention to them. Both boys shouted for them to come to play and Chrissy and Thomas got up. He turned to Chrissy briefly, touching her hip. 'This is the beginning, Chrissy,' he said, his hungry gaze making her blush wildly.

Fun was had with the boys and AJ and Jo returned to the poolside. 'I'm getting dressed and off for a nap,' said Jo as AJ came back into the pool.

'Why don't you two have a steam?' she said to Thomas and Chrissy. 'It will be relaxing – we have added some apple essence.'

'Come on, Chrissy,' said Thomas, as he struck out for the stairs.

Chrissy looked at the boys, and AJ said, 'Don't worry, I'll bathe them and get them dressed. I'm sure I'll find all Nico needs in the changing room, right? I also suspect that the boys will soon be in the land of nod given this afternoon's exertion.'

'Yes, thank you, AJ, I really appreciate it,' Chrissy said, watching as Thomas walked up the stairs. Jem and Jon made noises about going to Jem's allotment and Chrissy followed Thomas to the steam room. Chrissy was nervous as she entered the room. Surely this was too much of a risk.

They had both expressed their attraction to each other, and now she felt the desire building up within her.

She closed the door behind her. Thomas was standing in the steam room when she came in. The air was heavy with steam and a lovely light apple scent.

Without a word he approached her and took her hand, placing it on his chest as he moulded her hips into his. She could feel his growing desire. She was so very soft to his touch and she shivered as he held the small of her back fast towards him. His other hand travelled to her face and caressed her cheek. His thumb traced a soft pattern across her cheek as the rest of his hand held the back of her head. He moved her head towards his to kiss her gently on her lips. It was a feather touch that lit a fire within her. Thomas felt the heat rise within his manhood as he began to stiffen. This woman had such a profound effect on him. His kiss deepened as his tongue delved into her mouth, seeking out the outline of her teeth and exploring her mouth. Chrissy pushed back with her tongue, becoming an equal player in this game of desire. She raked her hands through his hair and pulled his mouth closer to hers, pushing her body into his further.

The most intimate part of him yearned to bury itself within her, but he had to slow down for her. He wanted to please this woman and satisfy her fully. His fingers moved along her spine, and his kiss left her mouth to trail kisses down the side of her neck, and she shook with want. His hands drew the straps of her costume down her arms and peeled it down a little further. She was naked from the waist up as he stood away for a second, unable to take his eyes off her pert breasts, only to then bow his head to one breast to lick the nipple while his other hand caressed the areola of her other nipple. He lifted his head to her ear and rasped, 'Chrissy, I want you; do you feel the same? I'll stop if you want me to'.

'No, please don't stop, I want you too,' she gasped as he jerked her upward and turned the dial on the wall to reduce the steam pressure.

'At this rate, I think we are generating our own steam and I need to see more of you,' he said. He stripped off his trunks and with one swift downward motion he pulled her costume down. She stepped out of it and kicked it away as he sat down on the seating against the wall, inviting her towards him. His fingers connected once again to hers and he tugged at her hand. She resisted and knelt in front of him, widening his legs. She trailed her fingers along his inner thighs until they reached his manhood. He drew in a breath. She was enjoying the power she had over him. He reached out to touch her shoulder and she sat back.

'You're not allowed to touch me yet,' she whispered, seeing the shock in his eyes turn to devilish humour at her teasing. She wanted so much to please him. She trailed kisses along the path her fingers had just traced and then her tongue darted out to lick the tip of his manhood before she trailed kisses up and down it. Thomas gasped as he hauled her up and sat her astride him. He was mad for her and she for him.

She was startled by this and drew her body back as if stung as he pulled her to him. Her opening was being nudged apart by his desire. He brought her a little closer, but not close enough to penetrate her. She couldn't wait – the voice in her head screamed and he plundered her mouth further. She was dripping wet with desire. He slowed the pace gently, pulling her body closer and kissing her as she kissed him back, more gently this time. The kiss grew stronger in force but still, he was restrained, not trusting himself not to lose control. He loved the feel of her supple breasts against his hair-matted chest and lowered his head to take each breast in his mouth one after the other. Her nipples were as hard as rock. He didn't know how long he would be able to hold back, he thought, as she kissed his neck and caressed his back. He placed his hand between them and touched her hood; she was so wet. His desire heightened as he delved his fingers further between her lower lips and made circular motions that had her thrashing around in his arms.

'Please, Tom, please, now, please,' she begged. 'I don't want to hurt you,

Chrissy, I want to be gentle,' he whispered.

'Tom, you won't hurt me, I'm stronger than you think.'

With that, he shifted her slightly and she felt him slide gently into her, draw back, and then invade her body with a long, hard thrust. Her world seemed to pivot at an angle and she felt like she was hovering. Her pulses were racing as he pushed in and out of her. Her own body thrusted back and joined in with his rhythm. It was as if they were one and a spell had been cast.

Chrissy's warmth engulfed his shaft and he lost this sense, his body, and his mind on a timeless journey with her, feeling weightless with heightened feelings, both heading towards a crescendo. They found their own rhythm and pace as they listened to each other's bodies.

'I want to come soon, Chris,' he rasped.

'Me too, please come now, Tom,' she breathed, as they both reached the for the height of their desire that, once ascended, would release them. They both held on tight to one another as wave after wave of sensations hit them and their minds exploded into a thousand little fragments around them, leaving them to shudder back to earth, their bodies jerking in satisfaction for this primal release.

Chrissy sat astride him for several minutes afterwards, Thomas whispering sweet words into her ears. 'You were so sweet, and I loved that.'

'Did I satisfy you?' Chrissy asked nervously.

'Are you serious, Chrissy?' Thomas chuckled. 'You shook my world, can't you tell?'

Chrissy knew they had both enjoyed their lovemaking but thought she may have been too inexperienced for Thomas.

He held her face in his hands. 'Chrissy, never doubt me when I say that was one of the most beautiful experiences of my life; Chrissy, trust me.'

She suddenly became shy, and made to move away and put her costume back on.

'No, let's just be,' Thomas said, holding her body to his as she lay her head on his chest, both of them breathing a little more evenly now.

He was caressing her back and waist as his thumbs began smoothing over the sides of her breasts. She felt her nipples harden as he held her back, and both his hands covered her breasts softly at first and then firmly. His eyes gazed into hers intently, the naked desire requiring satisfaction. He once again suckled her breasts one after the other, this time applying a little more pressure when Chrissy moaned, 'I like that so much.'

'Oh so do I, Chris,' he whispered. He began to harden again as she felt the corresponding desire flare awake within her again. The desire between them was irresistible. This time he thrust into her without further warning as they answered each other's call, thrust for thrust. It was like a madness that had to be quenched. He could not get deep enough into her and so he rose to his feet and moved to the opposite wall, holding her firmly to him, her back to the wall and her legs clenching around his hips. He invaded her body time and time again as she bucked and thrust back, until they were both spent and once again strove to climax and reach the heights of ecstasy. Chrissy lay her head on his shoulder, exhausted, as he held her tight against him. 'That was beautiful,' she said.

He looked at her and pressed a gentle kiss on her nose. 'It was.'

They stood for a while, foreheads touching, and their hunger assuaged for the moment.

Thomas poked his head out of the steam room and around into the pool house. Nobody was there. Both of them were naked as he effortlessly lifted Chrissy up and walked with her to the ladies' changing room.

He deposited her in the shower cubicle and she assumed that he was showering too until she saw his outline watching her through the glass door. He opened the door and stepped in, massaging the shampoo into her hair and smoothing it into the top of her head. He then took some shower cream and lathered it into her skin from her feet to her head and watched as it trickled away under the shower water. She tried to return the favour by lathering the shampoo into his hair but he was too tall for her to reach, so he lifted her into his arms just under her buttocks as she lathered the shampoo into his head. She felt the sensation of his tongue circling her nipple and gasped as he once again began suckling her breast. He slid her down and they kissed slowly. He turned her around so her back melded into his body and began to kiss her neck as the shower sprays cascaded down on them. His hands found her breasts again and began to cup them firmly, his kisses still leaving a burning path down her neck. Chrissy jerked as he once again found an erogenous zone on her neck and he revelled in the discovery, concentrating on that point as he quickened between his legs. 'Now, please, Tom,' she begged, as he tilted her slightly away and felt her wetness between her legs. He lifted one of her legs and entered her swiftly from behind while simultaneously quickly circling the nub between her legs to heighten her pleasure, which in turn led to another hurtling encounter back to earth as they both clung to each other beneath the shower sprays.

They applied shower gel again and touched each other gently as they went on a journey of unhurried exploration. They dried each other with the towels. Thomas went to collect his clothes from the men's changing rooms and returned. Chrissy felt bereft during those moments of his absence. He returned and they both dressed in silence, their eyes not leaving each other. Once they were fully clothed, he sat down on the bench in the changing room and pulled her down to sit on his lap. He held her and she rested her head on his chest. She wished they could stay like this forever. Who knew if this would ever happen again? He was a gentle and considerate lover, but their lives and lifestyles were so different and they were such different people, inhabitants of different worlds. She would treasure this time she had with him. She was in love with him. She knew that and was thankful that she would have at least have known this type of love once in her life. She would not of course proclaim this to him. It would embarrass him and prove her to be a simpleton, and Thomas may feel an obligation towards her. Of course, Chrissy had had sex before and had two very short relationships, but never had the pull had been so strong.

Thomas held Chrissy in his arms and felt that this was the woman he wanted in his life. She was the real deal and he would do whatever it took to fasten her to him. They could be a family, what with Nico and his mother and father. He would take it slowly and he would make himself irresistible to her. He extricated himself from Chrissy's arms and set her on her feet. 'We should see what's happening around the house,' he said, immediately feeling the cocoon around them shift to allow others in.

'Yes of course – and Nico,' she agreed as they set off towards the door to the house. Chrissy felt a little stiff, as she had not had a relationship in a long time – and that had been a marathon session which she would not change for the world.

They entered the kitchen as AJ put the dinner rolls in the pantry to prove. 'Hello, you two,' AJ welcomed them. 'Bet you are relaxed now.'

'Yes, thank you,' Chrissy said, her cheeks flaming as if AJ might have guessed what had just transpired. Could AJ tell that they had made love? Chrissy and Thomas exchanged an enquiring look.

'I've made the custard, and now over to you for the lasagne,' she said to Chrissy. 'Tom, my boy, you're on apple crumble and salad too.'

Thomas nodded.

'Adda boy,' AJ said as she left, knowing that Thomas was up to it as she had shared many a cooking lesson with him and Nicholas as boys.

Thomas went to grab Chrissy just as AJ popped her head back around the kitchen door and raised an eyebrow. 'Nico and Jamie both fell asleep in the silver room playing with the baubles in there – they were pooped. Jo's in her room and Jem and Jon are discussing politics and dozing in the library.' With that, she was gone.

Chrissy and Thomas both laughed as AJ now knew something was going on between them. 'So, you cooking?' asked Chrissy.

'Yes, me – I'll have you know that many an afternoon were spent in this very kitchen with Nicholas, learning to cook with AJ.'

Chrissy was surprised; Thomas wouldn't have struck her as someone who would be comfortable in the kitchen, but looking at him now, nothing would be more fitting as he went about finding all the necessary ingredients that they would need for their respective dishes. He conjured up two matching burgundy aprons and placed one over his own head, tying the back, and then over Chrissy's neck, before tying the back and then snaking his arms around her waist and kissing her neck.

Chrissy quickly detached herself from him. 'Anybody could come in, Tom,' she said, scandalised at the prospect of Jo, Jem or Nico finding them in a compromising position. Thomas made a chicken noise and flapped away from her, laughing.

They worked in harmony and Thomas could not resist touching her or kissing her neck as he passed or at intervals that suited him. Chrissy's cheeks flamed as he suggested that the apple sauce would be better eaten off her navel. They had various discussions while they cooked and found they agreed on many topics of the day, with not much disagreement.

Jo was the first to come into the kitchen. 'The smells coming from in here are lovely! So, who is doing what and can I help?' she asked.

'No, Ma it's all in hand,' said Thomas.

Jo teased that she could see that fun was being had, by the look on their faces. Thomas looked in the mirror to see that his forehead and cheek were swiped with flour. Jo raised an eyebrow, indicating Chrissy's backside, which had a handprint in flour too.

'Mother, what can I say? I can't keep my hands off her,' said Thomas, with a strait-laced expression. Jo felt a mixture of shock and relief. There was affection between these two, or was it something more, she thought.

'Jo, why don't you sit down and we can have a chat while Tom and I cook,' Chrissy suggested, pulling out a chair and trying to deflect attention away from herself. As Jo went to sit down, the doorbell rang.

'Who can that be? We're not expecting anyone, are we?' Jo said as she made her way to answer the door.

'Tom, you've got to stop with the teasing – people will get the wrong idea,' Chrissy chastised, to which he quickly retorted, 'Or the right idea!'

He moved to spoon her and wrapped his fingers around hers, stilling the movement by stopping her fingers grating the cheese and rubbing his cheek against hers. A stubble was forming, which tickled Chrissy's face, making her squeal and giggle.

They heard Jo returning to the kitchen as she made a little racket to warn of her approach. As she entered, someone followed her in, with Jem and Jon behind them. Thomas refused to let go of Chrissy as she struggled for him to release her. Jo was not surprised, but Jem seemed to be.

Anne came up to Chrissy and Thomas. 'Ah, Chrissy, here you are,' she said, moving towards them. Chrissy released herself from Thomas and moved to the sink to quickly wash her hands, and before she knew it Anne was standing next to Thomas, whispering into his ear and then planting a lingering kiss on his lips. He draped his hand around Anne's waist as she turned to face them all. 'That should be me,' Chrissy's subconscious screamed. Jo frowned and looked disapprovingly at Thomas, while Chrissy felt like he had slapped her in the face. She stopped in her tracks to greet Anne, and lowered her head in shame, unable to look at Thomas or Jo. What was happening?

Jem mumbled something inaudible in confusion at seeing Anne, but quickly regained his composure by hastily introducing Anne to Jo and Jon. It was unusual for Anne to meet Chrissy and Nico anywhere. Did she really care for Nico after all? Was that why she was here?

'I'm glad you are here, Anne,' said Chrissy.

'Yes, I'm sure you are,' Anne replied, with a large dose of acidity. 'I'm lucky that Tom texted me the address or I would not have had a clue of where you were.'

Chrissy didn't know how to respond to that. Of course, Anne had been going out with Thomas. How could she have been so stupid? Anne was more in Thomas's league, with her sleek red jersey dress and stilettos in a matching vibrant shade, and her make-up expertly applied to complement her striking blonde hair and blue eyes. She and Thomas made a beautiful couple.

'Shall we sit, perhaps somewhere more comfortable?' Anne said, drawing Thomas with her away from the kitchen, as Jem led the way to the silver room.

CHAPTER EIGHT

*'T*his is all very odd,' muttered Jo disapprovingly as Jem, Anne and Thomas left the kitchen. Chrissy's heart was shattering, her tears waiting to be safely shed. She needed to control her emotions or risk behaving like a lovesick fool. Jo and Chrissy completed the dinner preparations and very little was said aside from banalities associated with the meal. She could tell that Jo was confused about Thomas's reaction to Anne and didn't know what to say.

Chrissy and Jo joined the others in the silver room. Anne was sitting snugly with Thomas on a sofa sipping a glass of wine as he caressed her folded leg. Chrissy sat on a chair next to the sofa on which Nico and Jamie were sprawled asleep. She looked down at them affectionately.

'They shouldn't be allowed to sleep there – no manners, really, darling,' Anne said to Thomas.

Chrissy sprung to defend them and herself. 'They are fine here – they are children, Anne, it's not about manners.'

'Yes, you would say that. I blame myself, really, but what could I do? Someone has to put food on the table. Well, all that will change now,' Anne replied.

If Chrissy wasn't mistaken, she could swear Thomas had almost spluttered on his whisky. What did Anne mean?

98

'It's clear that he needs a real mother's firm hand,' Anne said.

Chrissy was astounded by this, but would not quarrel with Anne. She had never expressed any interest in Nico and it was all very strange that she should do so now. Chrissy absent-mindedly stroked the hair away from Nico's forehead as he slept.

'It's perfectly fine, Anne,' said Jo, as Nico stirred.

'Mama!'

'I'm here, Nico dear,' Anne said as she rushed to his side.

Nico's eyes focused on Anne as she sharply cupped his face and grabbed his upper arm, almost lifting him off the seat. 'Mum? Where's Mama? I want Mama,' he said, his voice wobbling a little.

'Now, don't be such a brat.' Anne pulled his arm further and sat him upright, clearly causing him some discomfort.

Chrissy saw a slight movement from Thomas's direction as she released Anne's grip from Nico's arm, saying, 'Gently, Anne, Mama's here, darling.' She took Nico into her lap and leaned him towards Anne. 'Give Mum a kiss, Nico.'

Nico gave Chrissy an accusatory look before planting a forced kiss on Anne's cheek. He looked at Chrissy again, seeking her approval, and she smiled warmly at him.

'Yes, good,' Anne said as she walked back and deposited herself beside Thomas, whispering into his ear again, causing him to display a somewhat strained smile.

Jamie stirred at the disruption and awoke to make a beeline for Jon's lap. Nico gave Chrissy a wet kiss and nuzzled her throat as she swayed to and fro with him in her lap. Thomas was watching her intently, but his eyes hid his emotions.

'I slept a long time, Mama, I was very tired, but I had a lot of fun,' said Nico as he looked at all the other adults in the room.

'Do you think Grandma and Grandpa would like a kiss?' Chrissy whispered to Nico, and he nodded. He approached Jo and Jem and kissed them, and received hugs back as their eyes moistened with tears, their hearts full of gratitude at the happiness that had been afforded them. Nico approached Thomas as Anne grabbed his hand and pulled him into a brief hug. Thomas pulled him gently on to his lap, forcing Anne away from him and hugging Nico, who planted a kiss on his cheek. Nico's eyes fell on Jamie who was only just becoming fully awake. 'Can Jamie and I go and play?' Nico asked Chrissy. 'AJ left out a puzzle in the games room.'

'Of course, darling; do you both want a drink?'

Both little boys nodded and held hands as Jo led the way so she could turn the light on for them in the games room. Chrissy excused herself as she went to get a drink for Nico and Jamie.

As Chrissy was returning to the lounge, AJ followed her in. She must have put the dinner rolls into the oven to bake as Chrissy could smell the fresh bread baking. Jem began to introduce her to Anne, but AJ interrupted him, saying that she was 'just the housekeeper'. Anne snubbed her and did not even acknowledge her. Chrissy considered that AJ was quite shrewd and wanted to be 'undercover', so to speak, so that Anne would not know AJ's true place in this home and, true to form, Anne had behaved badly. Chrissy noted that Thomas and AJ had exchanged a coded look, with a slight nod from Thomas. Clearly, AJ was of little interest or use to Anne, but Chrissy was upset on AJ's behalf. AJ, on the other hand, did not appear to be in the least fazed and sat on the sofa that Nico and Jamie had just vacated. Thomas's expression remained unreadable throughout. It was as though he was deep in thought, his eyes expressionless.

'So, Anne, I hear you are a model' asked Jo, watching Anne as she stroked Thomas's thigh, this motion not going unnoticed by Jo, whose brows instantly knitted together in disapproval.

'Yes, I'm currently completing a contract for an Italian designer. The shoots have been in Morocco and I've been away for a couple of days.'

'Do you enjoy it?' Jo asked.

'Yes, it's all very glamorous and I get to travel a great deal. I'll also be auditioning for an exclusive contract that will require a move to Milan as the face of a leading cosmetics company. It will be a great move for Nico and I.'

Chrissy drew in a breath. This was the first she had heard of this, or any interest that Anne had in Nico.

'Yes, I've decided to focus on Nico and my role as his mother. And of course, Chrissy deserves to live her life without the encumbrance of a small child dictating her life.'

So that was that – Anne meant to take Nico and Chrissy was not part of the equation. Chrissy was crestfallen; she really had no desire to live with Anne, but Anne meant to take Nico away from her. Chrissy felt Thomas's eyes narrow on her as she lowered her head to hide her shock. Why was she even thinking of doing this? Chrissy was quite bewildered.

Thomas's heart ached at seeing Chrissy so hurt. Nico was her life. There would be little left of Chrissy without Nico. He felt powerless to help at the moment. Anne had him over a barrel at present as she was Nico's mother and could do whatever she liked; she could even cut Chrissy out of Nico's life. It was clear that Nico would suffer greatly, but he would have to adjust if Anne carried out her threat.

Jo and Jem could not hide their shock, either – just as Nico had come into their lives, so he would be gone.

'Oh, don't worry, Jo and Jem, we will arrange for you to have some form of contact, won't we?' Anne turned to Thomas.

'Yes,' he answered stiffly. Thomas could see that AJ was apoplectic with rage and he caught her eye again as he could see that her fuse was about to be lit. She took his warning to say nothing and kept a tight rein on her mouth, which was not one of her finer skills.

Jem spoke up. 'Shall we prepare for dinner, AJ?' he said, his eyes asking for abeyance from any outburst. AJ turned abruptly and stomped into the kitchen as Chrissy muttered an excuse and followed her.

In the kitchen, AJ turned to Chrissy and asked, 'What is going on here?'

'I don't know,' said Chrissy, sitting down on one of the chairs and biting her lip in confusion. 'Anne has never mentioned moving with Nico; that has never been the dynamic. I look after Nico and she concentrates on her work. She doesn't even live with us in the true sense of the word and just flits in and out of our lives as and when she pleases. I don't know what she is doing; I don't seem to feature in the future she is planning for Nico and herself.'

Chrissy's common sense told her that Anne's interest in Nico was not sustainable. Anne had too little to gain from it. Of course, Anne was Nico's mother and she could choose to do whatever she wanted with him, but what was driving her?

Chrissy put the lasagne in the oven and laid the table before going to the games room to tell Jamie and Nico that they would need to come to dinner in a short while. As AJ completed the finishing touches for dinner, she regaled Chrissy with tales from Nicholas and Thomas's childhood. Thomas had always been the protective older brother, only occasionally becoming embroiled in Nicholas's foolish antics. Yes, Thomas was still sensible, AJ assured her, referring to the dilemma that Anne had created. 'Don't you worry about it – Tom will find a way. Trust him, Chrissy?' AJ said pointedly.

If only Chrissy could be sure of that. Maybe she was being selfish, as one possible outcome would be for Thomas and Anne to get together and look after Nico. Though she tried to be happy for Nico, her heart was heavy for herself as she would not feature in this plan for Nico or Thomas, who had come to mean so much to her.

Chrissy sat next to Nico at the dinner table. Thomas and Anne sat next to each other across from her, with Anne continuously whispering into Thomas's ear and exaggerating her reactions when he would reply. Her hand would stray to his thigh and Anne would give him a wry smile. Chrissy could not help her thoughts reverting to their passionate lovemaking earlier that afternoon and she could not equate how the pendulum had swung so wildly away from her to Anne, whose feelings he seemed to invite and reciprocate now. Had their union meant so little to him? Everybody save Anne and Thomas seemed to be unnerved by this open display of intimacy, to which Anne remarked, 'As you all know, Tom and I have been seeing each other for weeks now.'

Jem nervously started to chatter. 'Tom, isn't there that dinner being held next Friday for old Cartwright's retirement and our pending merger? Considering that Chrissy is giving serious consideration to joining the firm again, she should attend with us, don't you think?'

Thomas opened his mouth to answer, but Anne interjected. 'A dinner, how lovely? Obviously Chrissy could come, but wouldn't it be more fitting that I go with you, Tom?'

He took a moment to collect his thoughts and agreed, contradicting Jem, which was a first, if Jem's odd look at Jo was anything to go by. 'Of course, you should come too, Chrissy, with the others attending from the firm,' said Thomas, as if it were an afterthought.

In one fell swoop, Thomas had shown Chrissy her place in his life. No place aside from the office. It was true that she would remove herself from their lives for Nico's sake, but she didn't expect it to hurt so much.

Dinner was an ordeal and Chrissy excused herself when AJ rose to clear away the dishes. She helped in the kitchen and then went to see how Nico was faring. It was getting to bedtime and Jon and Jamie were saying their goodbyes. Jamie and Nico hugged their farewells and excitedly made plans for when they would next meet. When they had gone, Chrissy helped Nico change into his pyjamas and encouraged him to sit with Jem and Jo to read a book from his bag. Nico always liked to carry a book and would often pull it out to ask to be read to, which usually fell to Chrissy. AJ excused herself for the evening and left.

Chrissy sat on the sofa opposite Thomas and Anne in the silver room. She could see Nico's eyes drooping as he became sleepy and his head nodded into Jem's shoulder as he desperately tried to keep awake. Both

Jem and Jo delighted in watching him nod off, Jem gently cradling him.

'Tom, would you be able to run us home soon?' Chrissy asked. 'Nico is sleeping and it's getting quite late.'

Thomas immediately rose to his feet, almost dislodging Anne from the sofa, which was quite comical.

Anne was not amused and flung at Chrissy. 'Must you be so tiresome? Interrupting such a perfect evening, and you, Tom, being such a gentleman – I'm sure your men could take her, we needn't disrupt our plans for tonight.' She pouted at an outraged Chrissy, and Jem nearly choked on the brandy he was sipping. 'Anyway,' Anne continued, 'only Chrissy needs to go home – Nico and I have no reason to leave.'

Chrissy was very upset, knowing that Nico would be too if that suggestion came to fruition. He had never been apart from Chrissy in his whole life.

Jo stood up as if she could no longer bear the way this conversation was going. 'Of course, Chrissy and Nico are always welcome to stay if they wish,' she said, before adding, purposely and rather begrudgingly, 'You too, Anne, but surely Nico will be upset without Chrissy. You surely know this?' Jo was trying to appeal to any maternal feelings Anne may have possessed.

'Of course, I hear you, but many things will change soon and the sooner Nico gets used to life without Chrissy the better,' Anne said, coolly.

Chrissy couldn't believe what she was hearing and stood riveted on the spot, her eyes filling with tears. She looked at Thomas but could not see his expression as her vision was blurred. She quickly walked to Anne and knelt next to her. 'Anne, you have every right to keep Nico with you, but don't do it so suddenly – he will be so upset.' Only Anne and Thomas could hear as she spoke in a very low, pleading voice.

'No, Chrissy, you've...'

Thomas abruptly stood up and cut Anne short. 'Well, Anne, it would rather thwart our plans tonight if Nico stayed,' he said, looking into Anne's eyes and tucking a loose strand of hair behind her ear affectionately.

Jem and Jo were now sitting talking with each other after Thomas had exchanged a look with them. It seemed they could not look at Chrissy; she felt beyond shame.

'No, Tom – Chrissy has become very selfish when it comes to Nico and it's not fair. He will stay with me! Chrissy, of course you must go home, as it is rather late.' Anne drove the issue home and would not be moved.

Chrissy got up and moved towards Nico. She stroked his hair and planted a kiss on his forehead. 'Night, Nico,' she whispered as he stirred. She turned away and started to walk towards the door.

Suddenly Jem's tumbler fell from his hand and hit the delicate side table, causing the glass top to shatter. The noise woke Nico, who sat bolt upright. Chrissy moved towards him, but Anne rushed to his side, crooning to him, as Chrissy diverted to Jem and asked if he or Jo had been hurt. She picked up the large shards of glass as Thomas also came over.

Nico started to cry and pushed back at Anne, who was trying to cuddle him. 'Mama, mama!' he cried, rubbing his eyes with damp knuckles. 'No, I want Mama.'

Chrissy went to Anne's side and said to Nico, 'Mum is here, Nico – look how she is looking after you.' She tried to pacify him, but to no avail. Anne moved away from him, and with a great deal of resentment allowed Chrissy to cuddle Nico.

After he had settled down, Chrissy asked, 'Nico darling, how would you like to stay with Grandma and Grandpa? Uncle Tom will be here too.'

'With you, Mama,' said Nico. How tuned in little children were.

'Well, Mama has to work but you can stay here. Mum will be with you too and she will look after you.'

Nico looked at Anne, and from the look in his eyes he was clearly not satisfied with this potential arrangement. He was about to protest, 'No, Ma...' but didn't finish.

'Now, Nico, you will listen to me?' Anne began as she meant to go on.

'We won't tolerate your nonsense any more – you are a spoiled little boy.'

As Anne spoke, Nico visibly took a breath in as if swallowing as much air as possible, and then exhaled a barrage of 'No's at Anne, pushing her away, and almost toppling her over.

Chrissy was stunned. This little boy who never spoke harshly had let forth such an avalanche of dissent, she was genuinely disturbed for him. She gathered him to her, despite his thrashing, which bruised her a little on her chest, and he slowly quietened.

Anne huffed as she withdrew from Nico. 'He needs to learn, Chrissy – next time you may not be here to deal with his tantrums!' she spat.

'Here, let me take him.' Thomas took Nico into his arms, and he did not resist.

'I may as well come along for the ride, Tom,' Anne said, following them.

Chrissy bid Jo and Jem goodbye and Thomas bent to allow them to kiss Nico.

'Now come back soon, won't you Nico?' Jem said, as Jo looked on and smiled. Both kissed Chrissy on the cheek and gave her an apologetic look as she walked away. Before leaving, Chrissy assured Jem and Jo that Nico had never had such an outburst before, and they understood immediately. Anne rushed to the car and seated herself first, as Jesse held the door open for Thomas to sit next to her and place Nico in the car seat opposite. Chrissy sat beside Nico as he held her hand for comfort. Chrissy was silent throughout the journey as Nico slept, although Anne spoke passionately about her latest fashion adverts and pending cosmetics contract.

Chrissy hardly slept all night. Thomas had carried Nico to their bed and sat and stroked his hair affectionately. When Chrissy had returned from the bathroom, he was still sitting on the bed, looking at Nicholas's photograph. As Chrissy entered the room, Thomas stood up and came towards her. Anne was collecting some things from her room. Chrissy turned hurt eyes to Thomas's face. His eyes seemed to drown in her gaze. He stood toe to toe with her for a moment, his forehead against hers, her eyes squeezed shut. He breathed in her ear the words, 'Chrissy, trust me.'

They quickly stepped apart as Anne entered the room. She was aware that she had missed something. 'Come on now, Tom,' she said sharply as she led him out of the door.

Chrissy did not know whether she could trust him. She had shared herself with such abandonment and without reservation, and she felt more than a little ashamed at how he may view her. What if he thought she regularly behaved like this with men? These tormented thoughts dominated her dreams and disturbed her sleep.

Mo had woken Chrissy at five in the morning when he had telephoned her worried that he would not be able to make it into work that morning. He had been at the accident and emergency department of the local hospital since three o'clock with his six-year-old son who had lodged something in his ear. It turned out to be sticky tape. Chrissy reassured Mo and told him not to come in that day. In all honesty, she was thankful to get out of bed as she had hardly slept. She got up to fill in for Mo and turned on the baby monitor so that she would hear when Nico made waking noises.

She had partially cooked the breakfast items that would be needed and ensured that all the salad prep and hot drinks machines had been filled and ready by the time Sandy arrived. Monday special was always spaghetti bolognese, which was fairly easy to prepare as well. Customers were soon arriving thick and fast, the cafe ebbing and flowing as they dealt with the morning rush. Chrissy and Sandy had checked in on Nico through the morning and he was still asleep at eleven, so Chrissy left Sandy to man the cafe as she went to wake him. Nico must have been exhausted, she thought, as she blew air into his lovely face, trying to wake him. He stirred and flung an arm out and turned on his other side. Chrissy used a strand of her hair to tickle his ear, and he swiped it away.

'Nico, Nico,' she gently whispered.

He lay on his back and without opening his eyes treated her to a sleepy smile. 'Mama.'

'Morning, darling, are you very tired?' she asked affectionately as she watched him wake.

'Mama, I was very tired from all the playing yesterday,' he said.

'Did you have a good sleep, darling?' she asked.

'Oh, yes, Mama,' he replied, his eyes fully open now as he fell back on to his bed. Then suddenly his eyes narrowed and he asked in a whisper, 'Is Mum here?'

'No, she isn't, but she really would like to spend more time with you, my darling. Won't you let her?' Before he could protest, she added, 'Isn't it important to be kind, darling?'

'Yes, Mama,' he said, knowing this was the right answer but not fully persuaded of it in this context. He was in a happy mood with no mention of the difficulties with Anne the previous evening.

Nico wanted to eat cereal today, so Chrissy made a deal with him, that he would also eat a piece of toast with juice. He finished his breakfast and Chrissy bathed him. Domino was in hiding, as Nico had got it into his head that she was going to get bathed today, which she was having none of. Wombie was retrieved, and installed with Nico colouring in his book while Sandy and Chrissy dealt with the lunchtime rush. As the day was coming to a close Chrissy cleaned the kitchen as Sandy tidied up the customer area, before they both sat down to have a well-deserved cup of tea. Nico ate a small helping of spaghetti bolognese, spilling most of it down his top. As he had woken up so late, his mealtimes were a little befuddled. Chrissy and Sandy discussed their visit to meet Nico's father's family, and they both said they were looking forward to a break when the structural works began on the cafe and flat.

'Uncle Tom!' shouted Nico just before the bell rang to announce Thomas's arrival. Chrissy stood up, surprised to see him there, as Nico darted from his seat to Thomas's side and was flung into the air as if he weighed nothing at all.

'Hi, buddy,' Thomas laughed, putting him down and coming towards

Chrissy as if to kiss her. She stepped back to avoid him, which did not go unnoticed by Thomas.

She said a hurried 'Hi' and blushed as he watched her, a sardonic smile on his face and eyes that sought her gaze. Chrissy deflected attention away from herself and introduced Sandy to Thomas who shook hands with Sandy as Chrissy tried to focus her eyes elsewhere, but nonetheless landed on his hands. Those hands that had so intimately explored every inch of her body yesterday. At that moment she was drowning in her longing to touch him and for him to hold her like he had yesterday, as if she was a priceless gift that was being cherished. His kiss had transported her to a world that only they inhabited, where his touch set her alight with desire. She wanted very much to kiss him, but she felt that it would be a mistake to invite such attention again, especially as Anne had so clearly staked a claim on him now. Chrissy had little doubt that she had no role in Thomas's future and all there would be left for her would be the role of a mistress. No matter what Anne believed of her, she could not do that to any woman. Hence there was no use lamenting over this, and she gave herself a well-deserved shake. Chrissy caught Sandy's gaze as she raised her eyebrows and winked at Chrissy in clear admiration of Thomas's many attributes.

He was dressed in a black suit with a blue silk chain-link tie on a crisp white shirt. Chrissy almost laughed as she noted that she was very much seeing him as a dish on a menu that she would love to devour. The tie accentuated his black hair and made him look all the more dashing, but so out of place in this greasy spoon. Her pulse quickened once again as she longed to reach out her hand and touch him, inhaling his scent. He was probably wearing the same fresh citrus aftershave he favoured.

As Thomas and Sandy exchanged pleasantries and Chrissy caught that they were discussing her hasty acceleration to chef duties today, her mobile started to ring. Nico ran to get her phone and answered, giggling, 'I am the man of the house, Uncle Will – I'll give it to Mama.'

It was Will confirming that the contractor had finished a job early and could start on the cafe on Thursday. Chrissy indicated to Sandy to wait as she bid Nico and Thomas goodbye. She and Will decided that the works could start on Thursday as the patrons had been warned of the imminent temporary closure. They agreed that the notice to patrons would be updated, and Will said the temporary flat was ready for them and he would be delivering the keys to her the following day and arranging removal.

Chrissy explained the plans to Sandy and they agreed they would verbally tell customers the next day, and amend the posters on the doors.

'I'll be with you shortly, Tom,' she said as Sandy left for the day.

Thomas and Nico were discussing superheroes of the canine variety and Thomas managed to include a few human ones too, as Chrissy put up the amended posters. She asked Thomas to lock the cafe front door for her while she ensured that all the appliances were switched off. 'Shall we go to the flat?' she asked, and they all headed upstairs, shutting off the lights as they went.

Nico headed into their bedroom and the toy trunk as Chrissy and Thomas went to the kitchen. Chrissy asked what had bought him to the flat.

'I thought I'd check in on you and Nico.'

Chrissy smiled. They had to be civil, she thought, but she found it so hard to switch off the feelings she had for him. Knowing that she seemed to have been a substitute for Anne was very hurtful, but she could not force deeper feelings from Thomas when there were none.

CHAPTER NINE

C hrissy entered the kitchen. She could sense Thomas right behind her as she reached for the coffee. He looked so very handsome. She made him a coffee and took a glass of cordial herself. She called Nico to join them and he came running in with Wombie. She made Nico a strawberry milkshake which he relished as he sat talking to Thomas, who removed his tie and put it into his jacket pocket. Nico had been showing him his truck and took to the floor to play out an imaginary journey with bells and whistles as he crawled around the floor with it.

Chrissy sat down with her cordial and handed Thomas his coffee.

'I know you said that your landlord had a flat for you to move to while this place is being renovated, but the solution of staying at our home seems a lot better – just hear me out, Chrissy,' he said, as she was about to interrupt. 'Anne has already decided to stay with us and you agree that Nico has missed out on more than four years of knowing his grandparents. You agree that he needs to become accustomed to them. Due to the way that you have raised him he has already established a degree of closeness with us, only having met us in the last few days.'

Chrissy opened her mouth to protest, but she knew he was right.

This was an exceptional opportunity for Nico to get to know his whole family as he was not in nursery yet and her work would not be an issue. Chrissy also harked back to what Anne had said about wanting Nico to stay with her. She somehow felt that Nicholas's family's involvement in Nico's life may act as a buffer against any whims Anne may have. Chrissy was for any action that would benefit Nico's life, but suddenly parting him from her would not be. Though it broke Chrissy's heart to think of Anne and Thomas together, this provided an opportunity for Anne to foster closeness to Nico so that if she pursued her wish to have Nico live with her exclusive of Chrissy, then at least he would be used to her. Chrissy felt very much a third wheel and did not doubt that that way lay heartache, but for Nico, she would have to go and stay with them.

'OK, Tom, yes, we will accept your very kind offer. I agree that Nico needs to get to know all his family much better and form bonds,' Chrissy said as she sipped her cordial, and Thomas nodded.

'When do you think you will be ready to move?' he asked.

'Well, Will said I should take the things I need and put the rest into one room which they can move as they work through the flat.'

'Why don't I help you and Nico out on Wednesday evening?' Thomas suggested, as Nico seemed to pick up on the word 'move'.

'Where are we going, Mama?'

'Well, Nico, we are going to stay with your grandparents and Uncle Tom while Uncle Will's workmen come and repair the flat and the cafe,' Chrissy explained.

Before she had finished, he was running a lap of honour around the kitchen, making Chrissy and Thomas chuckle. He said he had archive boxes at the office that he would get delivered for Chrissy to pack things into.

'Will you stay for dinner?' Chrissy asked, thinking it was rude not to ask, considering that it was getting to that time.

'No, Anne – I mean, I am out to dinner with Anne tonight.'

Chrissy wondered if she imagined him stumble on his words.

'Oh, OK,' Chrissy replied. 'Of course, that's what normal people do, go out for dinner, not jump into the nearest steam room for some steamy sex!' Chrissy muttered under her breath, as Thomas wondered whether she had said something and held her eyes enquiringly.

He drained his coffee and placed the mug in the sink before heading to the door holding Nico's hand. He knelt beside him. 'So, buddy, I'm excited that you'll be staying with us for a while.'

'Me too, but...' Nico hesitated.

'What, buddy?'

'Does Mum have to stay too?'

'Ahh,' Thomas began.

'Nico, that is not on,' Chrissy interrupted, scowling at him and then at Thomas for giving him the green light.

'Sorry, Mama,' Nico pouted.

'And,' Chrissy asked, 'always be kind...'

'And if you can't be kind, be quiet,' Nico finished off.

'Good'. Chrissy indicated that the topic was closed.

Children's perceptions of people are driven a lot by instinct, and as Anne did not emit warmth towards Nico, and often did not even acknowledge him, he had clearly picked up on it.

'Uncle Tom, we have to bring Domino and Wombie too,' Nico said.

'Yes, of course, you can't leave without them. We will work it out. Now, bye for now, Nico,' said Thomas, ruffling his hair and picking him up for a kiss. He put Nico down, and Nico ran past them.

'Bye, Uncle Tom, I'm going to put Wombie to bed now.'

Thomas turned to Chrissy, who was standing behind him. 'Chrissy, I...' he began as she leaned forward to kiss him on the cheek and lightly touched his arm. 'Chrissy...' He groaned and pulled her towards him, his palms open and spread around her waist. Her soft body was sculpted to his hard hips and chest as he held her fast to him. She smelt the coffee on his breath as his mouth hovered above hers. His citrus scent made its way through her senses. His eyes were glinting like ice. He lowered his hands to her hips to better fit her to himself and then moved them to the small of her back, all along their eyes locked. He slowly lowered his lips to hers, laying soft butterfly kisses on them, and his tongue trailing a path to her neck and then kissing the side of it. Chrissy knew she should call an end to this, but she couldn't help herself or the fire that ran through her veins when he touched her. A fire that burned for him. His lips returned to hers as he gently kissed her. Her traitor body kissed him back with fervour as their kiss intensified. Her hands ploughed through his hair and travelled to his muscular back. She could feel his member harden with desire as she writhed passionately against him and his hands purposefully moulded one breast with his hands as his other hand rushed to lift her T-shirt up. She was equally rough pulling his shirt loose from his trousers, his buttons popping before she bent her head to lay kisses on his chest.

He looked down the corridor – no sign of Nico. She undid his belt and pulled down his trousers and boxers, and he lifted her clean off the ground and carried her to the kitchen unit, propping her up on it. His hand pressed down on her one breast as he pushed her skirt up, allowing himself access to her innermost recess, moving the crotch of her panties to the side. 'I have to have you now, Chrissy – are you ready, Chris? I don't think I can wait,' he groaned.

Chrissy showed him that she couldn't wait either, grabbing his fingers and guiding them to her opening, which was so wet for him. 'Now...' Chrissy shivered, sliding her bottom lower on the unit, allowing him to enter her in one swift movement. Chrissy threw back her head in triumph as she gyrated against him and he drove deeper and deeper into her with each thrust. They travelled together to a destination that was unknown, and where the only thing that mattered was this journey and this moment. Each thrust made them crave more and then with one final thrust she was shaken to her core and overcome with pleasure so deep it left her empty of everything except her passion for him. They both climaxed and jerked as the final throes of passion tingled within them.

Thomas held her to him and gently kissed her closed eyes and then the tip of her nose. It was after some time that they turned their attention to the sight they must be. Her top was pulled up over her breasts and her skirt was riding around her hips. His trousers and boxers were at his feet and three buttons had popped in the middle of his shirt. They inspected themselves and burst out laughing, but ceasing almost immediately, knowing that this would lead to Nico running into the kitchen to find them in flagrante. They moved apart; Chrissy slid off the kitchen counter and each righted their clothing. Thomas was first to be as decent as possible; he stood watching her and she returned his gaze.

His mobile phone rang at that moment. 'Yes,' he answered. His body immediately stiffened. 'Yes, yes, I'm just leaving the office – I'll be there in an hour.'

It was Anne, Chrissy thought, bringing her back to earth with a thud. It was clear that Chrissy had her uses, but so, it seemed, did Anne. Chrissy felt she had no right to ask any questions. He had made her no promises and they had undeniable chemistry. She could not judge him or herself. She did, however, need to call a stop to this madness, didn't she?

'Tom,' she said moving away from him.

'Yes,' he said, reaching for her hand. She let him take it.

'This feels wrong, Tom,' she said. 'I mean, you are with Anne, and –'

'Look, Chrissy, I do try to stop myself when you are near, but I can't. I know it's not fair on you, but resisting you is impossible. I can promise to try to stay away from you and I know what you mean, but the situation is delicate. I am not in a position to clarify everything to you...'

He tailed off after saying so much, but at the same time not saying enough. He had expressed his desire for her but also reflected the questionable morality of it. Chrissy was none the wiser about what his position was, only that it was jumbled.

'I'll go, Chrissy,' he said, kissing the tip of her nose. 'But know this,

I have feelings for you.' And with that, he left, closing the door gently behind himself.

Thomas sat in the car for a few minutes looking up at her door, feeling close to her here, and not wanting to leave her. He gave the signal to move and Ryan started to drive. As the car passed the changing landscape from town to greenery, his thoughts puzzled over the solution to his dilemma. He was in no position to explain his situation with Anne to anyone. His family knew him and were content to leave him to resolve 'Annegate', as AJ liked to call it, but Chrissy may not be able to trust him. If he disclosed his plan to Chrissy, he felt sure she would be torn between doing what was right and her loyalty to Anne, so he had to act in secrecy and await one final piece in the puzzle that he hoped would fall into place soon. He had to keep Anne sweet for just a little bit longer. Chrissy and Nico's futures were at stake. As he was driven home, he could only imagine the torment that Chrissy would be going through as she would see her intimacy with him to be a betrayal of Anne.

Thomas had some archive boxes delivered to Chrissy the next day for her packing and removal. Anne did not have very much left in the flat, but Chrissy packed it all into a box to take to Jem and Jo's. The best part of the day was spent packing, which just left the larger pieces of furniture in situ. Mo and Sandy ran the cafe without Chrissy. Anything perishable in the cafe would be taken home by them or taken to the local soup kitchen. By noon on Wednesday, all the packing had been done and the flat looked sparse. Chrissy and Nico sat on the sofa looking at how different the place was. The cafe had closed early today and Chrissy made her way downstairs to bed down the equipment and defrost the freezer. She waved Mo and Sandy off, ensuring that they would contact her should they require any assistance. They were being paid their full wages over the refurbishment period.

As she unscrewed the back panel of the freezer to get to the ice behind it, she gave some thought to assist in the criminal department at Waite and Sons. Staying at Jem and Jo's she would have no overheads and they would not accept any money for their board, but she could feel she was contributing if she did help at Waite's. It was with this thought, then, that her decision was made in the affirmative. Chrissy's hair was all matted with sweat and her clothes were damp, as the fluid from the freezer had bled on to the floor where she had been sitting. She really could have done with a shower but Thomas was due to arrive and all their things had been packed away. She picked up a cardboard piece from a dry-goods box that she could sit on in the car.

As she walked up the stairs to the flat, her mobile phone rang. It was Will asking if everything was OK and whether she needed help moving. Will already knew she and Anne would not require the flat as they would be staying with Nico's grandparents. She also felt honour-bound to tell Will that she would be working at Waite and Sons as they would not take any money from her for their board. She wanted Will to know that he need not pay her wages, but he would not hear of it. He went further and said that if she could find work in the legal field again for the future, she must go for it. He assured her that the flat would be her home for as long as she wanted and that her job was there *if* she wanted it and if not, he would work around it. Chrissy was touched by his kindness. Will was like a guardian angel and sometimes she felt like he had been sent by her late parents to care for her and Nico.

Nico sat with Wombie on the sofa as Domino snuggled next to him. Chrissy looked at him and there seemed to be a finality in their situation that she could not understand; it was as if this was an end of a chapter somehow. Nico jumped up, Wombie hanging from his hand, as Thomas rang the bell. Chrissy answered the door, making sure Domino did not run out as there was no way of knowing when she would be back and she had yet to be bundled into her pet carrier.

'How have you been, Chrissy?' asked Thomas, his eyes drinking in the sight of her as it felt like weeks since he had seen her.

'Fine thanks,' she said as Thomas longed to take her in his arms and just hold her until her warmth permeated his very soul. She invited him in and he took in how empty the place looked.

'We have to take those boxes with us and I'll need to take that cardboard,' Chrissy said, pointing to the boxes in the lounge as they entered.

'Why cardboard?' Thomas asked.

Chrissy was a little embarrassed as she explained, 'Well, I am all sweaty and dirty from cleaning and defrosting the freezer downstairs, and there was no time for a shower. I'll lay the cardboard in the car to avoid soiling it.'

Thomas caught Nico's gaze and raised his eyebrows mischievously. 'Nico, what say we go and see how bad Mama actually smells?'

'Yesssss!' Nico screeched, as they both crept towards her.

'Don't you dare, guys!' Chrissy warned them, but they were undeterred and just kept getting closer. As they almost reached her, Thomas said to Nico, 'Wow that's really bad!' He waved his hand in front of his nose as if to ward off a bad smell and Nico collapsed into his arms, both of them laughing.

'You two are mean,' Chrissy mock-huffed as she folded her arms and stood firm.

They stopped laughing and Thomas, asked Nico, 'Does it matter that Mama is smelly?'

'No, Mama, we love you even if you smell,' Nico giggled, as Thomas high-fived him.

'Now forget about the cardboard, Chrissy – the car can be valeted if need be,' Thomas said, and that put an end to the ribbing.

Last but not least, they needed to pack up Domino. Chrissy drew Thomas's attention and nodded towards the cat. 'Nico,' Chrissy whispered, nodding towards the pet carrier, for him to open its door so she could grab Domino and push her in before she knew what was about to happen. Thomas looked on amused as Chrissy grabbed Domino with one hand and pushed her into the carrier, while her other hand closed the door behind her. Domino yelped and managed to connect a swipe to Chrissy's palm, which drew blood. Chrissy jerked back a little and inspected her palm, as Thomas and Nico gathered around her, alarmed. Thomas took her hand in his, looking for something to cover the bloody scratch, and sat her down on the sofa.

'Blood, Mama,' Nico said worriedly, coming to sit next to her.

'Ah, darling, it's just a little scratch, Mama is OK – look, Uncle Tom is going to make it all better.' She held Nico's concerned head to her chest and stroked his head with her good hand. Chrissy pointed out her bag to Thomas. 'There are some tissues in there,' she said.

He fished them out, and put one on her palm and gently pressed down.

'There are also antibacterial wipes, Tom,' she said.

He placed her other hand on her injured one and pressed it down as he retrieved the wipes too. He was impressed, but she could tell he was curious as to why she travelled with antibacterial wipes.

'Nico often has little injuries in the playground and so they are a must,' she said as he took a Wipeout and gently wiped the scratch for her. 'That's fine, Tom, thank you. Shall we make a move?' She got up, releasing her hand from Thomas's, and headed towards the boxes.

'Chrissy, why don't you give the flat the once-over and check that you haven't forgotten anything, and Jesse and I will move the boxes into the car?' said Thomas, as he picked up a large box and Nico went to follow him.

'No, Nico, you need to come with me, as Uncle Tom can't keep an eye on you and carry the boxes,' Chrissy said firmly.

'But...' Nico began to protest, and Chrissy tilted her head and raised an eyebrow. Nico knew Chrissy meant business.

'OK, Mama,' he said easily.

Once the rooms were all checked, Chrissy picked up the last box and made for the door. She put the box down outside the door to lock it as Nico stood by.

The atmosphere in the car was light-hearted and there was discussion about where they would be sleeping. 'I know that you and Nico share a room,' Thomas said to Chrissy, and then looked at Nico. 'Would you like your own room, Nico, or do you want to sleep with Mama?' Thomas gave Chrissy a reassuring smile.

Nico's eyes lit up and he gave the matter some thought. 'Mama, will you be able to sleep without me?'

Chrissy smiled at Nico, touched by this consideration, and Thomas had a satisfied smile on his face. 'It will be hard for me,' she said, 'but why don't we do this? You sleep with me and you can have your room too, and if you feel like you want to sleep in your room, you can go there.'

'That sounds sensible,' said Thomas, as he and Nico started making plans to redecorate one of the guest rooms to Nico's liking. They decided that choose a big bed in case Jamie had a sleepover too.

Chrissy did not feel awkward about this, as it was true that his grandparents' home would be a place that Nico would also call home as his contact with them increased.

Nico ran straight towards the kitchen as soon Jesse unlocked the front door, shouting, 'Grandpa, Grandma, AJ, where are you?', and shouts of acknowledgment came from the kitchen and the garden room. He found AJ in the kitchen and gave her a quick hug before bolting towards the garden room. Jo and Jem got up to welcome Nico. 'Nico, Nico!' they both crooned as they hugged him close. Chrissy greeted AJ, who met them in the garden room as they both walked in. She greeted Jo and Jem with a hug and thanked them for having them all while Nico excitedly filled everyone in on the plans for a room for him. He suddenly remembered that Domino was in the car as Thomas entered with the pet carrier. He set it down in a little annex off the garden exit where all her provisions had been laid out. Chrissy opened Domino's carrier and agreed with Jo that they should let her come out when she felt comfortable.

Chrissy excused herself to unpack and freshen up as she was all dirty from the packing and clearing earlier. 'Of course, my dear,' said Jo as AJ lead her to the hallway where Thomas and Jesse were bringing in some of the boxes from the car.

'I'm going to show Chrissy to her room,' AJ said to Thomas.

'Ah, yes, AJ, we thought Chrissy and Nico would share the room opposite mine,' he replied.

AJ raised an eyebrow, and Thomas continued, 'That will be until Nico's room is redecorated and then Nico can decide when he wants to move into it. There will be men coming in to start on the redecoration next Tuesday. Jesse, will you get the last box from the car and bring the rest of the boxes upstairs to the guest bedroom opposite mine,' Thomas asked as he picked up a box and began to follow Chrissy and AJ upstairs. 'AJ, I can show Chrissy to her room if you have things to do,' he said. AJ took up the offer and told her to freshen up and relax and not to worry about Nico as she went back to the kitchen.

Chrissy let Thomas lead the way around the landing and she was led to a room opposite his. He opened the door for her to walk in. It was simple and tastefully decorated in damask pink and white with fitted wardrobes and drawers. There was a table with a huge vase of lilies and two chairs, a little vanity table and mirror, and a two-seater sofa near a large window. It was spacious with a beautiful and tranquil vibe. Thomas went further into the room and opened a door on the other side that led into a bathroom that had a large bathtub with a large rim and a shower cubicle in similar colours to the bedroom. There was an array of shampoos and body washes which she was sure would make for a relaxing bath.

Jesse deposited the last of the boxes in her room and she asked him to take Anne's box into her room.

'It's so beautiful, Tom,' Chrissy said as she sat on the bed.

He came and sat beside her. Her pulse quickened as she steeled herself to resist him. He simply took her hand in his and planted a kiss in her palm where the outline of Domino's scratch was still visible. 'As are you,' he whispered, still holding her hand in his. 'Hey, are you up to date with your tetanus shots?' he asked, not really romantic now.

'Yes, this is not my first scratch from Domino,' she smiled, wearily.

'Look, I'm tempted to stay and have my wicked way with you,' Thomas said, looking at her intently, 'but you look so very tired.' A smile flickered on his face as he added, 'and you actually do pong a bit!' He dodged a punch to his arm. 'Make yourself at home, Chrissy – to be honest, I need a shower too, perhaps...' He tailed off as they both remembered the last shower they had had together. He got up and said firmly to himself, 'She's tired, leave her alone!' and he left the room, but not without a glance back at her as she wickedly lay back on the bed, resting on her elbows and giving him her best come-hither look. In a split-second his eyes darkened and he turned to come back into the room and ravage her, but she was too quick as she ran into the bathroom and locked the door, laughing with glee.

He tried the door, and said, 'That's your first pass, Chrissy and... there won't always be a door between us.'

That sounded very much like a promise, and Chrissy gasped. She opened the bathroom door silently a few minutes later and felt bereft as she saw the door to her room was closed and he was gone.

She wanted him with her all the time but couldn't risk it. He made her wild with passion where common sense and decency vanished and nothing was more important than being in his arms. She became aroused, sitting on her bed all alone with just thoughts of him. Chrissy shook her head, trying to clear her mind of visions of his naked rippling body covering hers and invading her most sacred place in a slow rhythmic motion.

Her body betrayed her, yet her mind fought the temptation to give herself to him. What a battle this was, Chrissy thought, as she slowly organised the boxes so that those that contained items she did not need right now could be placed on one side, and she unpacked a couple of boxes that contained her and Nico's clothes and placed them into the wardrobe and drawers. She left his toys in a box to the side and piled the books on the bedside table. On Nico's side of the bed, she placed the photo of Nicholas.

She placed her minimal toiletries and her perfume, her one extravagant luxury, on the vanity and went to have a shower. She had placed Nico's Superdog towel on the towel rack as well, ready for his bath this evening too.

CHAPTER TEN

*C*hrissy emerged from her bathroom more than an hour later clad in a large bath towel, having enjoyed a long, luxurious bath. She had intended to have a quick shower but had turned the bath tap on and added some peach bath creme. While it was filling, she had taken a quick shower to clean away the dirt and wash her hair, after which she had lowered herself into the bath. She had soaked and allowed her mind to rest, driving any controversial thoughts away from it. She couldn't remember enjoying any such moments of peace. Nico was taken care of and she had a little time to herself. She would deal with her issues with Thomas later. Now was a peaceful time. Chrissy walked to the vanity and brushed her hair, suddenly feeling so tired as if even the weight of the brush was too heavy a burden.

She went to the large bed and placed a pillow at a diagonal angle and draped her hair towel over it, and then just let herself fall face-first on to the bed. He feet dangled off the side and before she knew it sleep had enveloped her and pulled her into its soft folds.

Thomas had showered and gone to approve and amend a draft document in the library and emerged wondering where Chrissy was. The family was in the games room. Jo was reading. Nico and Jem were playing Monopoly and Jem could not afford to place a house on his purchased square. Nico explained that he could borrow from the bank and did not need to repay the loan. 'No, Grandpa, listen carefully, this is important,' Nico stressed. 'Grandpa, Mama says we should always help each other. You are not going to win this game and I am not going to win this game, Grandpa; we are going to just play, OK?'

Jem laughed and then became silent. 'Nico, my boy, I think you may have a point,' he said, entering into the true spirit of the game and deciding that they would do as they wanted, with community chests and chances being taken by agreement between the players.

Thomas popped his head into the kitchen and AJ confirmed that dinner would be in twenty minutes. He agreed to call Chrissy down and climbed the stairs to check on her. As he opened the door there was no movement in the room and there she was, sleeping on her stomach across the bed. His heart softened as he approached her silently and her face was turned away from him. He lay beside her and lifted her hair to expose the side of her face. He planted a light kiss on her shoulder and his fingers trailed a path down her back before the intrusive towel stopped the venture. He leaned on his elbow and stroked her arm. How could he be so at peace with someone, not saying anything and just being in her presence? This was a new feeling for him. Where did this sense of rightness come from? His interaction with other women had always been full of constant chatter and this was how he thought it always was, or was it? She slept in peaceful slumber next to him and all was right with his world.

Chrissy murmured something and turned on to her side so her back nudged into him as she snuggled closer to find a comfortable position against him. She seemed to slip back into sleep and he took the opportunity to kiss her exposed cheek. Her buttocks burrowed further against his groin sending an arousing sensation to the base of his shaft and flooding through it. What was he? A randy schoolboy turned on by the merest suggestion of intimacy? He chastised himself as he tried to think platonic thoughts and failed miserably.

Chrissy could feel something hard against her back. She wanted to move back, but couldn't. She pushed back a little as sleep diminished and her eyes opened slowly to take in her surroundings again. Yes, this was a nice place, what a lovely bath and how relaxed was she feeling now. She ought to get up, she thought, pushing back to lie on her back but was being prevented from doing so.

'Good evening, sleepyhead,' Thomas whispered, and Chrissy moved along a little to trace the voice and was met by his face close to hers as he turned her to face him. He bent his head to smell her shoulder. 'You smell like peaches... mmm...' he went on.

'You don't smell so bad yourself,' she replied, inhaling his citrus scent.

'Kiss me, Chrissy,' he asked, needing her to show him that she wanted him. She lifted her face to his and gently kissed the side of his mouth before slowly kissing him full on the lips.

He responded just as gently, kissing her back. 'Hmm...' he murmured. Their kiss was soft and gentle like a calm walk across a beach, a revelling in the simple things in life, Thomas thought, as Chrissy parted her lips from his to end the kiss. He rolled over on to his back and pulled her on top of him, her cheek on his chest, and they lay like that for a few minutes, saying nothing but feeling so much.

'We need to go for dinner,' he said, breaking the silence and kissing the top of her head.

'Yes,' she said, neither of them making any move to get up. After a few more minutes Chrissy lifted her head and planted a kiss on his lips before flattening her hands on his chest to heave herself away from him. Her towel was partially caught beneath him and she couldn't move further. Chrissy tugged at the towel as her eyes met his. Their eyes silently debated before he shifted his weight to allow her to tug the towel free.

'That's your second pass, Chrissy,' he warned, smiling – but meaning every word. He lay back and watched as she sat at her vanity.

'Tom, I want to get dressed,' Chrissy said, feeling strangely shy dressing in front of him despite him having explored her naked body intimately.

Thomas sighed in resignation, knowing that if he did not leave now, nobody would see them until tomorrow afternoon and that was something that could not happen yet. Chrissy was surprised that Thomas didn't fight her on this request and excused himself with a smile.

Chrissy dressed in a dark blue and white flowered skirt and a white T-shirt with blue espadrilles. Everybody was in the garden room and Nico was sitting next to Jem, enjoying a strawberry milkshake. They seemed to have a mutual adoration going, Chrissy thought, as she greeted everybody. Seeing Thomas with everybody else still reminded her of their earlier intimacy, but this was soon dampened as she noted that Anne was sitting very close to him.

'You tolerate him so well – you really are very good,' Anne remarked to Jem, regarding Nico.

Chrissy flashed her an angry look, making it clear that she did not appreciate these digs at Nico. 'He's my good boy, aren't you, darling?' Chrissy said, as she sat beside Nico and squeezed him.

Jem was already helping Nico to steady the glass in his hand. Here was Chrissy trying to nurture a bond between Nico and Anne, and Anne seemed hell-bent on destroying what tenuous existing connection there was between them.

Dinner was a pleasant affair as AJ had prepared tortellini in honour of Nico's arrival, and everyone seemed very hungry as the whole dish was demolished in no time. Nico was given some pieces of ham on a side plate to feed Domino as she laced through everyone's legs during dinner. Unsurprisingly she didn't approach Anne again after she had already kicked her away once. At Nico's request, dessert was ice cream, which he relished.

After dinner, AJ and Chrissy cleared away the dinner things and started tidying up in the kitchen. AJ said that Thomas had hired three permanent staff to do the housekeeping from Monday and she was delighted that she would have more spare time. She disclosed that she was due to retire this month and would relish just overseeing the running of the house after that. Chrissy was glad for her but worried that their presence may have added to the work. AJ told her to perish the thought as this house had mushroomed since Thomas had come to live here and it was just a matter of time that more staff would be needed.

Once Chrissy and AJ had finished the cleaning, they joined everybody else in the conservatory. AJ was explaining that the menus for the week were completed every Sunday evening and as Nico was here now, Jo had asked AJ to prepare the menus with Chrissy for the time being.

'That's not necessary, AJ,' Chrissy said.

'That's where you are wrong,' AJ said. 'An army needs direction and it makes my job a lot easier. I think it's a great idea.'

'If you think it is helpful, then I am more than happy to do it, but on one condition,' said Chrissy. 'I get to learn some of your delicious recipes. Those tortellini were so lovely – the pasta was so thin and the filling was divine.'

'Deal,' said AJ, and shook Chrissy's hand as she sat down.

Chrissy remained standing and addressed the family. 'We are so grateful to you all for allowing us to stay with you while the repairs are being completed in our home. I also see that it is an excellent opportunity for Nico to get to know you all better. We would like to repay you for your hospitality.'

'I'm sure that won't be necessary,' Anne said dryly, as Jem vetoed it straight away.

'Absolutely not.'

'There you have it,' said Anne.

'No, Jem, I insist, I just want you to consider something,' Chrissy said as Jem and Anne were about to interrupt again.

'Guys, let Chrissy speak,' intervened Thomas, gesturing to her to continue.

'Well, I thought as you won't accept money, which wouldn't be much, I would like to help you out. Jem, you said you could do with some help in the criminal department at Waite & Sons, and I'd be happy to do this. I would firstly like to do this as you've been so kind to us, but also because while Nicholas was with us his passion was the criminal department, and now he is no here I feel you would like to continue with this department in his memory. He was Nico's father, so it would also be for Nico.'

All except Anne and Nico appreciated this sentiment for different reasons. Jo and Jem were surprised, but strangely Thomas not so much. He had a satisfied look on his face. He watched as Chrissy had explained her reasoning. Somehow he had felt innately that it was important to let Chrissy say her piece.

'Chrissy, this means a lot to us,' said Jem. 'Of course, the firm does not necessarily need the criminal department to be profitable but we want to keep it very much alive for Nicholas. It was his baby. So, yes, we would very much like you to help us but I insist on paying for your work. No, let me speak now, Chrissy. It is you and Anne who have agreed to stay here so that Nico can get to know us and it has been you who has given up your freedom to facilitate our contact with Nico and, for that, we will always be grateful.'

Thomas was impressed by how his father had put it. 'That's settled, then,' he said as he got up. 'Also, Chrissy, there is a retirement dinner on Friday evening, and everyone in the office is attending, so you will need to come to that as well. Anne can look after Nico.'

The looks of horror on Anne and Nico's faces were comical. Anne stood up and walked towards Thomas and curled her arm into the crook of his elbow. 'I thought we had agreed that I would come too, Tom,' Anne drawled sweetly. As Thomas appeared to be about to protest, Anne put her finger to his lips and just 'shushed' gently, saying, 'It's for the best'.

Tom nodded. They agreed that Chrissy would start at the office on Monday and would travel with Thomas. In the meantime, Nico and

Chrissy could settle in here.

Chrissy could not make out what was going on. Anne and Thomas seemed to have some kind of connection or agreement that she could not make out. It just didn't make sense! AJ, Jem and Jo all piped up, confirming that they would look after Nico and that this was how the family worked. Chrissy had never felt so supported before. When it had just been Nico, herself and Anne, Anne had not really been in the equation and all plans would have to factor Nico in. Chrissy thought she would not want it any other way, but it was so unusual to have that choice to have others share the care and responsibility for Nico.

'Do I actually have to attend the dinner?' Chrissy asked.

'Oh, yes, my dear,' said Jem, 'the whole firm is going and I'd like George Cartwright to know the people at Waite & Sons and feel confident that when it comes to the merger, his firm is in decent and competent hands. Even I'm coming out of retirement for it!' he chuckled.

Chrissy nodded, understanding the need to attend and began to wonder what she would wear.

'It will be cocktail wear,' Thomas supplied as if reading her thoughts.

'Ah, you probably don't have anything suitable do you, Chrissy?' interjected Anne.

This was a rhetorical question, but Thomas tried to assist. 'Anne, she could borrow something of yours, surely?'

Anne pretended to splutter on her drink. 'Oh, Tom, how funny you are – you know full well that Chrissy is at least two sizes bigger than me. Sadly, she wouldn't be able to fit into anything I own and her feet are unfashionably large.' With that, Anne had reduced Chrissy's self-esteem to zero. Chrissy supposed that, compared to Anne's swan, she was a bit of an ugly duckling.

'Hmm, you are right, of course, Anne,' said Thomas, 'you have the advantage over Chrissy as you are the woman that many women want to be.' Anne preened beneath the weight of his compliment, and he went on, turning to Chrissy, 'but most men would choose Chrissy over a bag of bones any day.' Once again, Anne spluttered on her drink, but this time for real.

Chrissy was mortified for Anne and herself. Hadn't Thomas just hinted at something between him and Chrissy?

Jem laughed openly, looking admiringly at Jo. 'Oh, yes, my boy, your mother still has it.'

'You are incorrigible,' Jo said in mock admonishment. AJ just laughed and Nico had no clue what anybody was talking about, stifling a yawn as he sat back on the sofa.

'Well, it's bath and bed for you, darling,' Chrissy told Nico, and there was no argument from him today as the excitement and expectation of moving in with Jem and Jo had clearly exhausted him.

'Mama, will we read the book about the funny donkey?'

'Yes, darling – OK, let's go,' Chrissy said, holding her hand out to him.

'We'll look in later,' said Jo, as Jem nodded.

'Actually,' Thomas said to Anne, 'why don't you give Nico a bath?'

For the second time this evening, Nico and Anne exchanged horrified looks, though Anne quickly recovered her expression and pretended to love the idea.

'Yes, what a good idea, considering I will be raising him alone in the future,' Anne said, making her point to Thomas and Chrissy. Anne rose to her feet and looked to Thomas to get up.

Nico, however, stood rooted to the spot. 'No, I won't go, I won't,' he spat out, looking at Chrissy and appealing to Thomas. Chrissy looked at Thomas for help as Nico seemed to be heading for another meltdown.

'I'll come too and so will Mama,' Thomas said as he approached Nico and knelt in front of him. He asked Nico to bring his ear to his mouth. Chrissy was intrigued and Anne suspicious. Once Thomas had whispered into Nico's ear he rose to his feet, turning to Nico again and saying, 'Promise, right, Nico?'

131

'Yes, Uncle Tom,' Nico said obediently and walked to Anne and put his hand in hers.

'Honestly, Tom, you must stop bribing and appeasing him – you'll spoil him,' Anne said, holding Nico's hand ahead of herself as he led the way.

Chrissy didn't know what to make of it, but clearly Anne was serious about the future being more her and Nico, rather than Chrissy. Although the selfish side of her was upset, she had to admit that she had always wanted Anne to show Nico more love, so Chrissy was determined to nurture this relationship.

Chrissy was about to sit back down when Thomas asked, 'Chrissy, do you mind sorting out Nico's nightclothes?'

'Of course,' Chrissy agreed, as she bid the others goodnight and followed them to her room.

Thomas and Anne took Nico into the bathroom. Thomas was conversing with Nico, asking him which bubble bath he wanted, and had started to run the bath and pour the bubble bath in. Nico said he would not take his clothes off until Anne left the bathroom, and he demanded his rubber toys. Anne came into the bedroom, already annoyed, and Chrissy sat her down and spoke to her in hushed tones.

'Anne, Nico just needs to get used to you, and you need to be patient.'

'You've spoiled him, Chrissy.'

Chrissy got up and selected Nico's bath toys and handed them to Anne, who carried them into the bathroom. Nico was already in the bath, covered with bubbles and brushing his teeth, and the next fifteen minutes were spent with Anne squealing with annoyance as she was splashed time and time again. Chrissy had laid out Nico's nightclothes as Thomas came in, carrying a very pleased and noisy Nico in a towel. It seemed that Thomas and Anne were much wetter than Nico.

Anne was not best pleased and made to walk out of the room, but was stopped by Nico sweetly asking her to read him a book. Thomas winked at Nico as he made the request and the request itself infuriated Anne.

'No, I've had just about enough of you for one day,' she said angrily, as she stormed out of the room. Both Thomas and Nico fell about the bed laughing and high-fived each other. Nico squirmed as Chrissy made to grab him and he finally became still.

'So,' Chrissy asked them both, 'what was all that about?' She looked from Nico to Thomas but neither said anything.

'Sorry, Chrissy, we can't – we have a promise to keep' said Thomas.

Chrissy knew she wouldn't get anywhere with them and so sat Nico down once his pants and vest were on.

'Darling,' she said as he leafed through a book and replied, 'hmm'. 'Look at me, Nico,' she said, and he looked at her. 'What must we always be?'

'Kind,' he said as Thomas looked on.

'And?' Chrissy urged further.

'Respectful,' Nico finished.

'And, Uncle Tom, you will remember that too,' Chrissy said, exasperated at them both, as Thomas saluted her, making Nico giggle.

'Were you kind and respectful to Mum?' Chrissy asked, feeling a triumphant moment about to appear but, to her amazement, Nico quietly said, 'but Mama, Mum is not kind or respectful to me,' and lowered his eyes.

Chrissy was struck by this reality – the pain in his eyes, and the solemnity of his tone. He was right, wasn't he? Shouldn't a child be treated kindly and respectfully too, especially by his mother? 'Nico, you are right, darling,' she said, her eyes tearing up too, 'but, my love, will you try for me?'

'Yes, Mama,' Nico agreed as Chrissy pulled his top clumsily over his head to inject some humour back into the conversation.

'Now, no more sadness,' Chrissy said with a smile. 'Now go for a wee and pick out a book'.

Nico immediately picked out the funny donkey book and asked if Thomas could stay and read with them. Nico knelt by his bed for his

133

message to Nicholas and Thomas followed likewise, both facing the bed in the kneeling position. Chrissy watched them both with pride and let them have this moment. Thomas bowed his head like Nico and listened to Nico as he spoke to Nicholas telling him about what they did today and their new home for now. He extolled the virtues of the newly discovered members of his family and promised that he had been good. He admitted being a little mean to Mum, but said he knew Nicholas would forgive him. Thomas smiled at this. He could almost believe that his brother was listening from wherever he was, given the conviction with which Nico was addressing him.

In the end, Thomas read the book to Nico as Chrissy went to the bathroom to get ready for bed. Both Thomas and Nico were giggling at donkey's antics in the book as she came back into the room. Chrissy was wearing a white cotton nightshirt that was thigh-length and had pink piping on the edges. She looked ripe to be ravished, Thomas thought, but he reminded himself that she was probably still very tired after spending the day packing. Nico watched Chrissy get under the covers with him and cosied up to her while plonking his head down a couple of times on his pillow to get comfortable.

'Mama, sing to me,' Nico said, his voice dreamy now.

'No, Nico, go to sleep,' Chrissy said.

Nico raised sleepy eyes to hers and begged again, 'Please, Mama, I need one – the *Beauty and the Beast* one, Mama...' Thomas looked on with amusement as Chrissy warned him not to laugh.

Chrissy lent back on the headboard and pillows and began the gentle song, low and slow, while stroking Nico's hair. Thomas watched her as she sang quietly, as she watched Nico and Thomas. Her voice was soft and melodious and Thomas was entranced, just watching and hearing her as she smiled, a little embarrassed. Her eyelids began to droop ever so slightly as gradually a word was missed, then a couple of words until she missed whole swathes of the melody and finally nodded off to sleep mid-song. Thomas ensured Nico was in a comfortable position to sleep and went to Chrissy's side of the bed. He slid his hand under her legs and back and moved her lower into the bed so that her head lay fully on her pillow. He kissed both Nico and Chrissy on their foreheads and left them to sleep. He looked at them one last time before leaving the room and thought, 'This is my life,' as he quietly closed the door.

'Mama, I need to go wee,' Nico said, waking Chrissy from a deep sleep. Chrissy looked at her phone; it was one o'clock. She got him out of bed and took him to the bathroom before settling him back to sleep. Chrissy felt thirsty and left her room to go to the kitchen for a glass of water. It would also be good to have some in the room in case Nico got thirsty. She quietly opened her door. She was just in time to see Anne emerge from Thomas's bedroom. Chrissy was shocked and upset, not expecting to be faced with this reality that she had been grappling with. Anne was wearing a skimpy red negligee and clasping a red silk gown to her neck, and her hair was a mess as if she had been dragged backward through a bush – or thrashing on a bed, Chrissy thought, a slight tremor on her lips. They had just made love – Chrissy knew it.

Anne put her finger to her lips, indicating that Chrissy should not make any noise. She took Chrissy's hand and led her into her room, which had clothes strewn all over the place. 'I wanted to talk to you alone, Chrissy, so this is fortunate,' Anne said. 'I know Tom and his family are too decent to raise this but they never intended for you to come and stay here with us. Tom and I are trying to be as sensitive as possible but we are so drawn to each other he can't keep his hands off me. So, we are reduced to sneaking into each other's rooms and catching time with each other when we can.' A little colour came to her cheeks. 'We even have to resort to seeing each other at the office. His parents don't approve of me, but once Nico is comfortably settled and you go on to live your life, we intend to tell the old people to get used to Tom and I being together, but Chrissy – Tom

135

finds it terribly embarrassing when you seek out his company and use Nico to spend time with him.' Anne looked into Chrissy's eyes to make sure she was getting the message loud and clear. 'He doesn't want to hurt his parents' feelings by openly rejecting you, and he feels that you are trying to wheedle your way into all their affections when you don't actually belong here.' Anne finished with a frown on her face.

Chrissy was crestfallen – she couldn't believe this was how Thomas and his parents felt, but Anne's words rang true. After all, Chrissy had no place in this family, really, did she?

Anne continued. 'Tom is very much trying to see if he and I can make a go of it together for Nico's sake. Nico needs a family in every sense of the word.'

Chrissy listened, her soul dying with every word Anne uttered.

'You see, Tom has asked me to marry him and this is why I want to get to know Nico better and care for him myself. I know I didn't want to have anything to do with him before, but this is too good an opportunity to miss for Nico and I. Tom feels responsible for you and, whatever may have passed between the two of you, his primary concern will be Nico and me. In effect, I'm asking you to assist in Nico getting used to me and then disappearing so that we can make a go of things as a family. You do want this for Nico and I don't you, Chrissy?'

Chrissy was silent. She loved Thomas, and she thought he had real feelings for her, but this didn't seem to be the case. Also, of course Anne was Nico's mother and so she was the real link between Nicholas's family and Nico. Only Anne was the answer to the future of this family. Anne was right – Chrissy was endangering any secure future that Nico may have.

'You must promise to support me so that I can start a new life with Nico's family,' said Anne.

Chrissy considered this and nodded. No matter how hard it was, she had to make this happen for her Nico. 'Anne, you must promise me too that you will be kind and patient with Nico,' she insisted.

'Of course, I'll try, Chrissy, but he is a terrible bore,' Anne protested.

'He is what it is all about,' Chrissy said, with finality.

'Yes,' Anne said. 'Oh, and Chrissy, don't make a fool of yourself over Tom. All those sheepish looks at him – everybody is laughing at you.'

Chrissy rose from her seat, considering Anne's words, each one striking a shameful blow to her. Was she being so foolish? For Nico's sake, she needed to rein in her feelings for Thomas and try to make sure she was not alone with him.

With that, Chrissy left Anne's room. Once in bed again, sleep evaded her until the early hours when it brought with it a harrowing nightmare of being pursued and being unable to open many doors to escape.

CHAPTER ELEVEN

The following day Chrissy and Nico awoke late. They knocked on Anne's door and tentatively entered as there was no reply. Chrissy thought it would be a good start for Nico to get used to saying good morning to Anne, but before he could say so Anne yelled at them to get out. Chrissy explained to Nico that Anne must be very tried and that they should not have disturbed her. There was no actual sign that Anne seriously wanted to take over caring for Nico and her usual position of deferring care was still the status quo. Ah well, the day was still young, Chrissy thought, as she and Nico walked down the stairs. Thomas had gone to the office and AJ was baking bread. They sat with Jo and Nico and discussed the menus for dinners until Sunday and Nico clearly had a lot of input, as jelly and ice cream made an appearance on that day's menu.

They both had breakfast and followed Jem to his allotment after they had booted up and trudged through Jo's flower garden as she was weeding. She showed them where she had planted the jasmine that Chrissy and Nico had bought her, in pride of place at the exit of the garden room where its heady scent would greet them every day when it was in flower. Chrissy needed to keep her mind occupied to avoid thinking about a future not only without Nico, but also Thomas. This saddened

138

her immensely but she had heard that motherhood was sometimes about heartache. They worked all afternoon with Jem, helping him to harvest his courgettes, red onions and cherry tomatoes. Jem also showed them how to propagate some flowers, which Nico loved. He had never had the chance to garden at home as there was no outdoor space. As they worked, the radio played songs that they sang along to. Surprisingly, Nico taught Jem how to dance to a popular song that required jumping around and other easy moves. The afternoon was full of laughter, and at one point they stopped for a break for a picnic lunch of sandwiches made of fresh bread and various fillings. There were also crispy choux pastry buns filled with cream and topped with chocolate ganache. Nico ate three buns and would have eaten more if Chrissy hadn't stopped him. 'Darling, you will have a tummy ache if you eat more than can fit in your little tummy,' she said.

Nico remembered his last upset tummy when he hadn't taken heed of Chrissy's advice and so now he wisely stopped eating the buns, saying to AJ, 'I will have some later if there are any left, OK?'

'Sure it's OK, Nico,' said AJ.

Chrissy and Nico showered afterwards due to the amount of mud their bodies and clothes had attracted. Chrissy assisted AJ with the preparation of dinner, which was to be a chicken roulade with winter vegetables and the ice cream and jelly. Chrissy was fascinated to learn the technique that AJ would apply to create the roulade, and there was the sublime smell of a bakewell tart emanating from the oven.

Anne had not surfaced until the afternoon and had eaten something in the kitchen, refusing to come into the garden as she was wearing heels. Jem and Nico had gone to visit Jon and Jamie and said they would be back before dinner, while Jo had gone for a nap.

Anne called for a taxi in the late afternoon and said she was off shopping for Friday evening. Chrissy thought about what she would wear as well. She had a couple of dresses that would be suitable, Anne would be flabbergasted to discover. The remainder of the afternoon was spent fully unpacking and stacking the archive boxes in the garage, some of which could be reused. She put Nico's books in an orderly fashion and made a mental note to herself that Nico would need a bookshelf in his room.

Thomas arrived home early, greeting AJ and Chrissy as AJ tutored her on binding the roulade. Chrissy was concentrating hard to ensure that the stuffing stayed within the flattened chicken and was succeeding until Thomas entered the kitchen and stood next to her. He looked so very handsome dressed in a charcoal three-piece suit. Chrissy admitted to feeling a little jealous of Nico as he launched himself into Thomas's arms. This movement, along with her lack of concentration, knocked her elbow, which didn't assist in the aesthetics of the dish.

Nico was chattering about the fun he had had with Jamie and that he was going to sleep over at Jamie's tomorrow. Nico turned to Chrissy and said, 'Grandpa said I could stay if that is OK with you, Mama.'

'If Grandpa says it's OK, then that's fine, darling,' Chrissy said, finally rolling the roulade the best she could. Thomas was standing so close to her that she could smell the familiar citrus of his aftershave and she found it hard to concentrate or will her hands to follow AJ's instructions without shaking a little. He radiated a kind of heat that fogged her mind. Chrissy cursed her traitorous heart, which would not see reason and recognise that she would jeopardize the secure future for Nico if she gave in to temptation.

'That's not bad for your first attempt,' said AJ, snapping her out of her daydream. She wrapped the roulade into the cling film and placed it into the refrigerator.

'I'm going to change – is Anne in?' Thomas asked, and was told by AJ that she had gone shopping for a dress. Chrissy's innermost voice was telling her that Thomas just was not the type of man who would be involved with two women at the same time. He just wasn't, but her mind was screaming at her to stop being an idiot and not to ignore what she was seeing. She was confused yet he need only reach for her than her body felt compelled to respond.

Anne made it back for dinner and the evening was spent pleasantly with Jem teaching Nico about chess. Nico was engrossed in the way the pieces moved and asked many questions, the most frequent one being 'Why?' and the most frequent answer from Jem being, 'Because those are the rules of the game, darling.'

Thomas and Anne had retired to the library, Thomas making it clear that they wished to be alone, which hurt Chrissy, but this confirmed what Anne had told her – that she and Thomas were making a go of things. She decided she must now concentrate on Nico being without her and that she must fasten his attachment to Jem and Jo at least. She felt confident in their care for him and also Thomas's love for him. Realistically, Chrissy could not trust Anne alone with Nico's well-being as she was too selfish, but with this family's support, Anne could make a go of ensuring Nico's future happiness and health.

AJ and Chrissy had formed an easy-going relationship, and Chrissy learned that AJ had never married. She had two sisters, nieces and nephews who had children who lived in Brighton and ran a hotel near the seafront. She said she usually went on holiday there and very much enjoyed holidays away alone or with solo traveller groups. She had a great love for old buildings and architecture, which Chrissy shared. AJ regaled Chrissy with stories about the ruins in Paphos, Cyprus, and in Italy, Greece and Turkey, to name a few. Chrissy was enthralled; she felt she would very much like to visit these places and asked many questions.

Unbeknown to them Thomas was standing at the kitchen door listening and thinking about the simplicity in Chrissy's joy compared with the sophisticated things that made Anne happy, and her manipulative nature. He was struck once again by the difference between both cousins. He knew that he and Nicholas were very different, in that Nicholas had been carefree and very much a spontaneous personality, whereas he was a little more reserved and needed to consider and plan any actions. He liked for things to fall into place as he planned, rather than take risks. When considering this, he thought that he and Chrissy were also very similar. He hoped that Anne would make up her mind about what she wanted rather than changing the goalposts, so that he could plan a future too.

The following day was laid-back, as it was the day of the retirement dinner. Anne had met Thomas for lunch and it was also the day of Nico's first sleepover with Jamie. It was also the first time he would be away alone without Chrissy, and it didn't seem to faze him. He didn't often cry when he awoke in the night but she wasn't sure how he would be if he was in a strange place. She had put a slip in his pocket with her mobile number on it in case he or Jamie's mother, Erica, needed to call her. She packed a small bag for him with Wombie and two of his most favour-ite books, before walking with Jem to Jamie's house. Chrissy met Erica, who was a nervous little woman with mousy hair and delicate features dressed in jeans and a blue gingham shirt. They had a drink in the garden while Jem and Jon discussed Jon's broad beans. Erica was very indulging of the little boys, incessantly talking to them and asking them questions, and they enjoyed the attention. Jem and Jon exchanged a roll of the eyes over her chatter.

Chrissy and Jem returned home in the late afternoon. Nico had hurriedly said his goodbyes to them, very excited about his stay with Jamie. Erica had arranged a tennis lesson for the boys, which they were looking forward to, and Chrissy left her contact details.

Jo and Chrissy had helped each other pick out what they would wear that evening, Jo choosing a black velvet gown with some sparkle. She was a very handsome woman and, what's more, she knew it. They discussed the dinner and Jo explained that the staff at Cartwright and Co were all very down to earth, save for George Cartwright's son Ian, who was a junior partner in the firm. Ian was angling for a senior partner position once the firms merged. Luckily George had not made this a term of the merger, knowing that Ian's role in the newly formed firm may not be a good fit for his cavalier style of business. Thomas had his eye on him.

Chrissy was surprised to see that Thomas had returned home with Anne that evening. 'Well, I just need to agree with it, of course, and I'm not really sure it is right yet, Tom,' Anne was saying as they entered the garden room where the family was sitting. Anne's laugh was acidic in tone, and Thomas was nodding his head in a pensive motion. The family had been discussing how quiet it was without Nico bombing around the place. Thomas approached Chrissy and sat on the arm of the sofa where she was sitting, and asked where Nico was; Chrissy reminded him that he was at Jamie's for a sleepover. AJ had retired for the evening and left a selection of sandwiches and a Victoria sponge for them in case they were hungry. Anne watched Chrissy and Thomas, narrowing her eyes disapprovingly before announcing that she would be getting ready for the evening.

Jem and Jo excused themselves, leaving Thomas and Chrissy alone, and Chrissy stood up to follow them. Thomas put his hand out to stop her leaving the room. 'That's no way to greet a lover, Chrissy,' he said, his eyes teasing her. 'See, I'll even close my eyes if it helps – just a little kiss to tide me over till tonight,' he whispered as he watched her face flush.

He stood in front of her, and Chrissy could see she would have to give in to be able to pass. 'OK, close your eyes, then,' she said, and he immediately complied.

Chrissy quickly kissed his cheek and ran around him, and a chase ensued. She was clearly out of shape as he quickly caught up with her, grabbing her wrist halfway up the stairs. They laughed as he allowed her to escape, saying, 'Third pass, Chrissy.' There would not be many more passes, his eyes warned her, as she walked up the remaining stairs to her room.

She dressed with a care that she had not taken in a very long time. She showered and creamed her body and then donned a lacy black strapless bra and matching panties. She had also slid on a pair of black stockings with a red seam at the thighs. On top of her sexy lingerie, she and Jo had decided on a fitted black strapless dress. The cut was simple and tasteful but striking. Chrissy felt very daring as the dress defined her every curve and exposed just enough cleavage and leg to leave little doubt of the treasures that lay beneath the silky fabric. It ended just above the knee, allowing the beholder a view of long legs clad in black stockings planted in pair of stilettos. She looked at herself in the mirror and smiled, biting her bottom lip, feeling that the dress may be considered a little risqué. For jewellery, she wore a simple silver necklace with a large silver teardrop pendant and small matching earrings. She had straightened her hair so that it hung like a smooth curtain around her face. She applied her foundation and a plum lipstick and was satisfied with the look, which was completed by a small silver clutch bag.

Chrissy left her room. She saw that Thomas, Jo and Jem were waiting at the bottom of the stairs talking. Chrissy's heartbeat seemed to increase and rung in her ears as she descended the stairs, watched by Thomas. His eyes were hooded and started a slow journey from her stilettos, up her legs, past her hips and breasts to rest at her eyes. Her face was simply made, the skirt of her dress lifted each time she took a step down the stairs giving him a glimpse further up her legs and a flash of red stocking seams. His heart missed a beat and he drew in a breath. All he could imagine was how he would pull them down to expose her hot flesh. He longed to run his tongue up her legs and feel her shiver beneath his touch. He remembered the silky feel of her skin against his as they had made love and how soft and welcoming her body had been; her feather-light touching when she explored his body and the way she clutched his biceps as if she were stopping herself from drowning in the depths of their shared passion. He longed for that fulfilment again and stood helplessly, almost unable to move.

Chrissy mirrored the want in his eyes as she observed him too. He was dressed in a black suit with a black bow tie and white shirt. It showed off his tanned complexion and sculpted his muscular form. She longed to rush into his arms and just be held by him.

Thomas noticed that Anne had started down the stairs and sadly she had to be the focus for the time being. He felt like he had been doused with a cold shower and dragged his gaze away from Chrissy, now concentrating on Anne as she made a beeline for him. She was wearing a gold-sequinned cocktail dress that draped across to her side of her waist, with gold dangling jewellery too. Anne quickly overtook Chrissy and walked in front of her towards Thomas, holding out her hand for him to take. He kissed Anne's hand and asked her to go to the car.

Chrissy walked towards Jem and Jo, who greeted her with a kiss and complimented her on her dress. Anne gave them an aloof greeting as she passed them to go to the car. Thomas was behind Chrissy and stopped her, holding her elbow as they all started to make their way to the cars. He held her back, her back against his chest, and quietly whispered into her ear. 'You look incredible tonight, Chrissy. I wish we could cancel the dinner and go back to my room. Say you'll come to me tonight, Chrissy?' He held her shoulders to him and planted a sensual kiss on her neck, refusing to let her move. Her hand covered his briefly as he tightened his hold of her shoulder. 'Promise me, Chrissy!' he demanded.

She yearned for him. This last time she promised herself. 'Yes,' she breathed, as he released her, gently satisfied that she would make good her promise.

Jem and Jo had been driven in a car by Ryan, and Anne, Chrissy and Thomas sat in the second car, driven by Jesse. Anne sat opposite Chrissy and then pulled Thomas to sit beside her with little resistance from him. 'Chrissy, you really know how to cramp a girl's style, don't you? Why ever didn't you go to Jo and Jem's car?'

Thomas flashed her an angry look as he was on a call. Chrissy was silent and considered it was just Anne being her usual vindictive self.

The paparazzi were waiting as their car arrived and Anne stepped into the flash of camera lights, holding her hand out to Thomas. He gave her a little push so that she moved on, and then pulled Chrissy out of the open door and pinned her to his side while he flashed a smile at the waiting photographers. Chrissy only just managed to hide her bewilderment and gave a polite smile. No doubt their photograph would be plastered on various papers tomorrow. Chrissy was confused by Thomas's actions – surely Anne was the future? Anne was outraged and she was sure that Chrissy would pay for this later.

The retirement dinner turned out to be quite a smart affair and everyone was mingling, with cocktails and hors d'oeuvres circulating. On entering the banqueting rooms Jem introduced Anne and Chrissy to George and Ian Cartwright. Jem introduced Chrissy as the new manager of the criminal department at Waite and Sons. George greeted her warmly, pressing a kiss to her cheek, and she exchanged a handshake with Ian.

'I'm sure we will get to know each other better,' Ian said, rather lasciviously, and Chrissy almost replied, 'Not if I can help it,' but managed to stop herself before the words spilled from her lips. Anne, however, seemed to immediately warm to him as he invited her to get a drink, which she did, after she had darted Chrissy a venomous look promising retribution for Thomas's earlier slight.

Thomas asked Jo and Jem to excuse them while he pressed his hand gently into the small of her back and propelled her towards a group of loud people in the middle of the room. Upon seeing him approaching, the group immediately reduced their volume and turned to look at both of them. 'Some of you may recall that Chrissy used to work with Nicholas,' said Thomas, and several people nodded. Chrissy began to recognise faces from the criminal and commercial departments of Waite and Sons. Each person made a point of introducing themselves and those she knew reacquainted themselves with her. 'Chrissy is going to be managing the criminal department from Monday,' Thomas finished, and a whoop went up in the group as she was welcomed into the folds of the firm again. He began to speak to his colleagues and gave Chrissy a reassuring smile.

A young girl dressed in a plain black dress and black pumps who had not spoken to Chrissy yet came towards her shyly and said, 'Do you remember me, Chrissy?'

Chrissy honestly couldn't recall her.

'I didn't think you would,' the young girl said, with no hint of disdain. 'I'm Dina. I was work experience with Waite's when Nicholas passed away. I was mainly in reception for about a month.'

Chrissy began to remember a timid girl who wouldn't say much and was terribly shy, not much different from the girl in front of her today.

'Oh, yes, Dina, how are you?' Chrissy asked. Thomas looked over to her and gave her a questioning nod to ask if she was OK, and she nodded back.

'I'm OK, thank you. How are you?'

'I am well and quite excited to be coming back to Waite's,' Chrissy said.

'I've been working at Waite's since then and I'm still in reception and deal with post,' said Dina.

Chrissy felt Dina was hesitating before saying any more. 'What is it, Dina?' she encouraged.

'Well, I'm glad you are coming back. You were very kind to me,' Dina said. Chrissy didn't think she had been particularly kind, but she had treated everybody as considerately as she could. 'It's nice of you to tell me, Dina, thank you,' she said.

'I would like to work in the criminal department,' Dina said suddenly. 'I know I'm not trained, but I have been taking statements from clients for about a year now and I think I could do more – do you think I could help?'

Chrissy could tell that she was very nervous. It also seemed like someone was being quite cheeky in the criminal department and taking advantage of Dina by using her to do casework.

It was probably the first time that Dina had ever voiced an aspiration, and she seemed quite terrified. Chrissy put her hand around her shoulder and they both sat at a table that seemed to be the group's table. They turned their chairs to face each other so that they could talk properly. 'Look, Dina, I know that Tom would want to support you as much as possible in any aspirations you have to progress in the firm. Can I get to the firm and see how things are running, and if I see a possibility I'll consider it and we will see what we can do?' Chrissy lay her hand on Dina's hands, which were folded tightly in her lap. 'Dina, don't be nervous,' she said, her heart going out to the young woman, who looked about seventeen but must have been at least twenty-five. 'Now, I'm going to need your help to familiarise myself with everything I need to know at the firm, OK?' Chrissy said, wanting to boost Dina's self-confidence and clearly succeeding as Dina gave her a beaming smile.

Another woman approached, greeting Chrissy with a smile and hug. 'Welcome back, Chrissy,' she said. She was the main receptionist, Kam Kaur, and she had been with Waite's since Jem had opened the firm. 'I'm so happy to see you – we wondered what happened to you when you left.'

Chrissy explained that she had been raising her nephew and made general conversation. Her eyes looked for Thomas and found him searching the room for her as he had been circulating at the other end of the hall by now. Once he had seen her he walked towards her and pulled a chair out so that they could sit side by side, facing Dina and Kam. As soon as he saw Kam he kissed her on the cheek and asked after her, and he nodded to Dina to acknowledge her but he did not recognise her specifically. 'Tom, this is Dina,' Chrissy intervened. 'She works for us in reception and admin.'

Thomas stood up again, as did Dina, and he shook hands with her and apologised for not recognizing her. Dina blushed, as most women did when they met Thomas.

Thomas sat next to Chrissy and draped an arm around the back of her chair in a lazy fashion, leaning in to whisper to her and placing his other hand on her hand in her lap. 'Have I told you that you look beautiful tonight?' Chrissy too blushed as Dina and Kam smiled at each other and tried to excuse themselves. Chrissy got up and held both their hands, making them sit down again. 'Oh, no, you don't,' she said to them, and then to Thomas, mock-scolding him, 'You behave!'

'Yes, Tom,' Jo said as she came up and greeted Kam, and Chrissy introduced her to Dina. The gong rang for dinner as Jem joined them and they made their way to the dining hall, which was set in large round tables of fifteen people. There was no seating plan, as the thought behind the evening was to wave farewell to George, but also for the employees from both firms to mingle among themselves.

Anne was sitting at George's table with Ian and seemed to be enjoying herself. Thomas sat at a table with Chrissy, Nina and Kam and a couple of staff from the criminal departments at both Waite's and Cartwright's and chatted amiably. They were able to compare procedures in both firms and established that the two would probably be able to merge with little disruption. The topic moved on to personal life and family. It transpired that Dina was living with her boyfriend, who was not working at the moment, and Kam's kids had all left home and it was now her husband and her mother who lived with them. Her mother had problems with her sight and general wear and tear, as Kam put it, so she had many hospital appointments that ate up most of her and her husband's leave.

The menu was sophisticated and Chrissy complimented Thomas on selecting their choices. He smiled and said, teasingly, 'Well, I know what you like.' He wasn't just referring to the food.

There were speeches after dinner from George Cartwright and Jem, and then Thomas. George was met with a standing ovation and introduced Jem, who confirmed that of course Waite and Sons were affiliated with the Candour group headed by Thomas. He stated his confidence that when both firms merged and during the whole process the firm would become stronger and more prosperous. Thomas spoke about the future of Waite and Sons, and said that the merged firm would be called Waite's. He made a solemn promise that the future would be bigger and better for everyone, and it was only when everyone, including employees, was benefiting, that a firm could survive and prosper. Thomas added that he had enjoyed meeting many new people and he would like to get to know everyone who would work for Waite's, and hoped that the firm would be one where there should be a balance of work and play. He stated that the past five years and particularly the past few days had made him aware of what really mattered to him. It was family and being proud of what you did. He looked at Chrissy, Jo and Jem affectionately.

There was applause for all the speakers as the speeches ended and coffee was being served. Anne came to Thomas's side, placing her hand on his shoulder as Ian stood by. The table's attention was drawn to Anne as she bent to talk to him. Thomas turned to Chrissy and notified her that Anne had said she was not going to be returning with them. 'In fact, she doesn't know when she will be back.' Thomas didn't seem in the least interested, and muttered rather ominously, 'Oh, but I do, I do.'

Chrissy rose with Dina and Kam and they excused themselves to visit the powder room. Ian was standing outside and smiled at them as they entered. Anne was already in there, which would explain why Ian was hanging around, having spent the whole evening together. Maybe Anne has found another interest, Chrissy prayed. Anne was touching up her lipstick and looked at Chrissy in the mirror like she was something undesirable on the sole of her shoe as she entered a cubicle.

As Chrissy, Kam and Dina made to leave the powder room, Anne addressed Chrissy, spitting out at her, 'You will never learn, will you? You don't belong here.' Dina made a move to approach Anne, but Chrissy grabbed her hand to hold her back. Anne could be quite vindictive and just needed to be ignored, Chrissy thought. She couldn't have poor little Dina involved in this mess. Kam turned Dina around by her shoulders as they both followed Chrissy out of the powder room. Anne quickly followed on their heels and grabbed Chrissy's arm and spun her around. Ian was still standing outside, as were numerous other guests milling around.

Thomas and Jem were also passing and stopped at the familiar sound of Anne's voice, and the hum of the crowd died down. 'You know Tom is only using you for Nico and you're just his little plaything. Haven't you wondered why he was not interested in you when you worked with Nicholas and suddenly he is now interested? Well, you're a means to an end, aren't you, dear?'

Thomas and Jem were by Chrissy's side trying to gauge what was going on, and Thomas purposefully walked up to Anne. Chrissy held his hand and stopped him moving any further. She did not want this. Chrissy squeezed her eyes shut as Anne continued.

'Yes, ladies and gentlemen, listen – this is Tom Waite's whore... for now,' Anne said, as the crowd gasped.

Thomas tried to get Chrissy to release his hand, but she held on for dear life. 'No, Chrissy this won't happen,' he said. The photographers had got wind of a story and began to stand on chairs and flash cameras.

However, before Thomas could reach Anne, Dina walked up to her and though only slight she stood her ground in front of her, her feet planted firmly apart, and her voice loud and menacing as she ground out the words between tightly clenched teeth. 'I don't care who you are or who you think you are, but Chrissy is worth ten dozen of you, you evil witch. Don't you ever cross her path again!' And with that, she put a foot forward, which caused Anne to step back in fear. The crowd gasped again and claps rang out as Kam stepped in front of Dina, and Jem, Jo and other staff from Waite and Sons stood beside Kam in a warning to Anne not to come forward.

Anne was undeterred, and tried to manoeuvre around them to get to Chrissy. Thomas asked the shield of people to allow Anne to approach them as he stood in front of Chrissy and moved her a little behind him with one hand at her waist. Jesse and Ryan were standing either side of him and stopped Anne in her tracks by holding her upper arms. Thomas's voice boomed, and Chrissy had never seen him so angry before. 'Anne, you need to stay where you are. Be in no doubt that I will unveil you and your misdeeds right here in front of everyone.'

Anne looked around at the photographers and the crowd, her eyes revealing a conflict between common sense and vengeance. Jesse and Ryan were ready to lift her and take her away if need be.

Thomas continued, taking Chrissy's hand in his, and he brought her closer to him so that she was standing with one of his arms around her waist as close as she could be to him. 'I need you to know, Anne, and for that fact, everyone here, that Chrissy is the woman I love – and anybody that has an issue with her will have me to deal with. Also, Anne, I don't think you are in any position to call Chrissy names, when you have been all but trying to sell your son to me, as he is our Nicholas's son. I have all the evidence of this now and how unfit you are to be his mother.' Addressing the crowd, he added, 'I have an issue to settle with this unpleasant woman and I would be obliged if you could all go about enjoying your evenings while I do this in privacy. To the press, please let me have a few minutes – and this is your scoop: "Tycoon to marry the love of his life".'

Thomas kissed Chrissy's hand with a flourish, which was captured by all the cameras, and, with that, the crowds and press dispersed, save for Jem and Jo. Thomas turned to Dina and Kam and said, 'Thank you, ladies – you have proved yourselves to be true friends to Chrissy and, for that, we will always be grateful. Why don't you go to your seats and Chrissy and I will join you shortly.'

Thomas had said he loved her, Chrissy thought. That's all she could think. He loved her and he said he was going to marry her. Dare she believe this?

Thomas turned to Anne after the crowd had left. 'Now, Anne, you need be in no doubt that I do not want you and never have. I want you to never darken our door again. If you see us, make sure we don't see you. Now,

I'm willing to be quite generous but don't think you have a choice here. I had been trying to be civil with you for Chrissy and Nico's sake but I'm at the end of my rope with you now. So this is how it's going to work. You are going to sign the consent order that our respective lawyers have agreed and I will honour my end of the bargain, but I never want to see you around Chrissy or Nico. If for any reason you wish to contact either of them then you will have a way to do so, and Chrissy will decide whether she wishes to see you. When Nico is of age it will be his decision.

'I've been on a leash as far as you were concerned, as there was a little bit of information I was waiting for to ensure that you toed the line. I have video and audio footage showing you're effectively trying to sell Nico to me, and what I was also amazed to find was irrefutable evidence of exactly what illegal activities you have been involved in when travelling for your so-called modelling assignments!'

Anne gasped and put a hand to her chest. It would be true to say that she had not expected the latter bombshell and knew exactly what Thomas was referring to.

'Now, follow Jesse and Ryan, who will show you the evidence,' Thomas continued, 'and I will be happy to send you a copy but, in that case, I will also send a copy to the police. Please do not try me *ever*,' Thomas stressed. 'The sooner we tie up the consent order the better. I'll have your personal effects sent on to Ian's address.'

With that, he led Chrissy away, followed by Jem and Jo.

CHAPTER TWELVE

*J*o sat next to Chrissy back at the table, quite stunned by what had happened. Anne was at her most destructive, and Thomas had mentioned illegal acts and the police regarding Anne. Chrissy watched as Thomas was giving curt instructions to Jesse and Ryan, after which they marched Anne to collect her coat and led her out of the function rooms. Kam and Dina were already at the table and looked at Chrissy with concern. Chrissy gave them a weak smile.

Jo patted her hand and said, 'Chrissy, there is nothing for you to worry about. Tom has all this in hand and Anne won't be bothering you again. You know Tom loves you, don't you?'

Chrissy looked at her. This statement, which Thomas had also said, had washed over her and she couldn't quite believe it, but believe it she must. Thomas had expressed it in front of everyone. He returned shortly after and Jo moved to sit with Jem. Thomas gave Jo an affectionate peck on the cheek and stood before Chrissy, who was still a little dazed.

Thomas spoke to Kam and Dina, asking to see them for a meeting at Waite's at midday on Monday, and thanked them for caring for Chrissy, as he proffered his hand to Chrissy, saying they were leaving. Ryan would come back to collect Jo and Jem later. Thomas and Chrissy said their goodbyes to George and a few others before leaving. As they waited for

Ryan to bring the car around, they posed for several photos.

Thomas handed Chrissy into the car and then sat beside her. Ryan would be driving them home and closed the door behind them. Ryan notified that Jesse had Anne in hand and had triggered the privacy dividing screen up. Thomas sat back and pulled her towards him so that she was sitting well into the seat. He turned in the seat and tilted her chin to face him. 'Chrissy, know one thing above all – I love you. I have never loved a woman before and did not know what it meant before I met you. I'm no saint, as you know, but I've discovered love through you. I see how you love, it's in all you do for those you love. It drives you and it is you. I see how your love for Nico translates into your decisions and actions and how you instinctively react to situations. Love is giving yourself to someone without knowing where it will lead or whether that person will love you back and despite that.'

Chrissy couldn't believe what she was hearing; it was like a dream. 'But Anne said you had planned a life with her and Nico, and that you loved her and wanted to marry her...'

'Never. I was trying to get an agreement from her for the residence of Nico as she kept threatening to take him away from you and I couldn't have that. Those times she seemed intimate with me she was trying to see how far I could be pushed, and she could have gone on had it not been for my people finding out about how exactly she was making money. She goes on modelling assignments and was able to smuggle in drugs without being detected. I had been having her followed after I had recently run into her a month back and since then my people have been gathering information about her and all her trips and meetings. Finally, they were able to get video and audio footage of her agreeing to another importation and this is what I had been waiting for. It also helped that she was videoed trying to blackmail me into paying her large sums of money to have custody of Nico.

'She had already agreed in principle to a residence order for Nico in your favour via a consent order through her lawyers. This was in exchange for a sum of money, which I agreed. It wasn't how I wanted to deal with this, but I had to cut the cloth according to Anne's requirements. Now I also have the footage I don't think I have to pay her off but I want her to have some means. I have purchased a property for her in New York that she can live in for as long as she lives, on condition that she signs the residence order, and I will also transfer her a monthly allowance at my discretion. It was her choice where she wanted to live, and she chose New York.'

Chrissy was happy, but also very sad that her Nico meant so little to Anne.

'Chrissy, say something,' Thomas begged, holding her face in both his hands.

'Tom, I have loved you for so long – I don't believe you love me too,' she said, bringing her face closer to his, her lips seeking his for a gentle probing kiss. He kissed her back, igniting a fire within her. His tongue found its way into her mouth and explored its depths as her tongue played with his. Her fingers removed his jacket as he sat forward and she began to open his shirt buttons. In her haste, she fumbled and he ripped the shirt from his body, once again buttons flying off it. Chrissy wound her arms around his neck, bringing her body closer to his, as his fingers desperately sought a zipper for her dress. She moved her mouth away from his to giggle as he couldn't find a way to get into her dress, and she pulled her body back. 'Ah-ah,' she said tauntingly. 'You can't touch.' She put his hands by his side and held them there, enforcing her wish.

Thomas obeyed with excitement in his eyes as she leaned over him and kissed his cheek and began a slow trail of kisses down his neck and then nipped him on his neck. He drew a breath and Chrissy sat back in the seat, saying, 'I think that's enough for tonight.' He growled and went to grab her. 'No touching, Tom!' She lashed out her words and stopped his hands, his eyes pleading with hers. Chrissy could see that he was aroused and hitched her skirt up, exposing her black stockings, and lifted herself astride his lap and began kissing him. It was a long, deep kiss. She could feel his arousal but his trousers and her panties were stopping their union. Thomas thought he would go mad with desire as they felt and heard the gravel under the tyres heralding their arrival home. The car had barely stopped than he bounded out of the back of the car and bent back in to grab Chrissy out, before swinging her into his arms and running into the house and taking the stairs two at a time towards his wing.

She lost her shoes on the way up the stairs and laughed as he promised reprisals for her teasing. She bounced on to his bed and then landed on her stomach. As she righted herself, he rapidly disposed of his trousers, swiftly swearing while doing so. Chrissy couldn't stop laughing as he looked comical wearing just his torn shirt and socks. He fell into the bed beside her and she crawled away as he begged, 'No, Chrissy, please, I can't wait.'

'Darling, I need to be upright to unzip this dress.' She got to her feet and smiled, reassuring him as she pulled at her zip at her side.

He was beside her instantly and took over, pulling her zip down slowly down to her waist and bent his head to kiss her side as the descending zip exposed her flesh. Chrissy held her breath in and felt her body heat up with every kiss he deposited on her skin. The dress fell to the ground to reveal the lacy black bra and panties. Thomas drew in a ragged breath at the sight of the stockings and sat on the bed torturing himself while he drank in this vision that was his. Chrissy held his shoulders and then placed a leg on the bed beside him and bent slowly and purposefully, brushing her breast against his shoulder as she went to roll down one stocking. He stilled her hand and turned his head to kiss her inner thigh and draw one stocking down. She withdrew her leg and placed the other leg on his other side and he repeated the motions until both legs were free of the stockings and she stood in front of him.

He held her by the waist as if paralysed by desire and the compulsion to watch her as she leaned backward in his arms and then returned to push herself up against his chest. He took the opportunity to unhook her bra, which fell by her side, and watched her face as he took one breast in his hand and began to massage it and then massage them both in each hand. Chrissy held his head to her breast and arched backward, the passion becoming almost too much for her to bear.

Chrissy longed to feel his rough chest against her soft skin again and she stepped back, forcing him to stand, and removed his boxers, which slid down his legs. She reached for his hard shaft and began to move her hands up and down it until he shuddered. He ached and longed to bury himself deep within her. Thomas held her a little apart from him and then slowly and deliberately removed her panties. He bent his head to kiss the mound of her most intimate place and then went to his knees, parting her legs as he did so. His fingers brushed against her lower lips and one finger delved a little into the recess. Then again and next time a little deeper. He then used his fingers to part her lower lips while his thumbs rubbed the nub of her womanhood. He felt her knees begin to give way as she gasped. He turned her so that the back of her knees were pressed against the bed, and she fell on to the bed with a startled little cry. He returned to pay homage to her parted legs and slowly resumed worship at her intimate shrine. He parted her lower lips again and flicked his tongue at her nub and then opened her lips further as his tongue licked her in more forceful thrusts.

Chrissy lay back, thrashing her head from side to side and raking her hands through his hair, begging him to take her – she couldn't take it any more. He certainly was exacting his revenge for her teasing, by teasing her right back. Thomas looked up at Chrissy, satisfied that he had departed at least some degree of the pleasure she had given him and began to trail his tongue up her body.

'I can't wait,' Chrissy gasped as his arousal moved up her thighs and lay on her heated opening.

Thomas whispered in her ear, 'Chrissy, I love you my darling.'

'I love you too, Tom,' Chrissy replied as they met with one hard thrust, which filled her very soul and every vacant part of her being. She returned thrust for thrust with equal vigour as they both rode wave after wave of the desire that engulfed them. She pushed at his chest as she swiftly adjusted their position and sat astride him with hardly a break in their coupling. She rode him with abandon. Each of them possessed the other totally until there was just one of them moving in unison as they reached the crescendo of fulfilment, their shuddering bodies holding the wave until it crashed time and time again and all was still. Chrissy's body fell forward in utter exhaustion as he pulled her down by his side and cradled her against his chest. He kissed her forehead and held her to him, stroking her arm, her hand on his chest.

'Chrissy,' said Thomas after a while.

'Hmm?'

'You know we are getting married, don't you?'

Chrissy raised her head, lent her elbow on his chest and rested her face in her hand. 'You know you need to ask me don't you, Tom?'

'Chrissy, I promise I will, but please just say you'll marry me, my love, I will die without you.' He sounded genuinely bereft.

'Of course, I will,' Chrissy said softly, kissing his lips.

Although their desire would renew, they happily fell into a peaceful sleep knowing that they had each other.

$\mathcal{E}$PILOGUE

*T*homas did ask her to marry him the following week at a dinner at a fancy restaurant with the whole family there, including AJ, Dina and Kam. Nico had presented her with a simple platinum ring with a solitaire diamond that she had picked out days before, while Thomas got on one knee. She did say yes, as she had promised, and he rewarded her with a long, sensual kiss that had to be interrupted by a lot of coughing by Nico and Jem while the rest of the table fell about laughing.

The paparazzi had a field day, but lately Chrissy and Thomas didn't mind, making a display of themselves and obliging the photographers with photo opportunities, so that they in turn respected their privacy when asked.

Their wedding a week after that had been a small affair at a local church with just a few extra guests. Chrissy had worn a cream satin and lace knee-length dress with a short train and a silver and diamond-studded hair comb on one side of her hair. Her bouquet was of dark blue calla lilies. All the men wore charcoal morning suits with dark-blue cravats and kerchiefs and calla lily buttonholes – even Nico, who looked so very handsome. Will had given her away and had shed a tear at the wedding. He made a wonderful speech at the wedding breakfast remembering her mother and father and how proud they would have been today. Chrissy and Thomas had honeymooned in Rome, which had been a surprise, and although they spent a lot of time in bed, they also managed to visit many of the sites Chrissy had longed to see, with a visit to Pompeii being a highlight for her.

Life, since they had professed their love for each other, had been perfect. Thomas had shifted his work base to Waite's so that they could travel to and from work together. Anne had been paid off and she had signed the consent order that had conferred residence of Nico with Chrissy. Nico, unsurprisingly, was thriving in the bosom of a loving family, under the watchful eye of Jem, Jo and AJ. AJ had her helpers at home now and mainly supervised with Jem and Jo.

Life had settled into a comfortable pattern and Nico was getting excited about all the changes. It had been two months since the wedding and while the whole family had been sitting in the garden room on a Sunday Nico had asked a question of Thomas and Chrissy as they sat chatting to Jem and Jo.

'Uncle Tom?' Nico said tentatively.

'Yes, buddy,' Thomas answered.

'Gramps and I wanted to ask you a question and, well...'

'Go on, Nico,' said Jem supportively.

Thomas and Chrissy sat on the edge of the sofa and listened intently, Thomas leading Nico by his arm to come to sit on his lap. 'Go on, buddy,' he encouraged.

'Uncle Tom, can I call you Dad? I really want to.' Nico looked down at his hands, with which he was fidgeting in his lap.

Thomas looked from Chrissy to Jem to Jo and back to Nico. In all their eyes he saw consent and positivity. This is what I want and what Nico needs, he thought. 'I am so pleased, Nico. If that is what you would like, then you will call me Dad from now on, OK buddy?' His voice was heavy with emotion.

161

'I know that Nicholas is my real dad,' said Nico. 'I will never forget him and we all miss him but you are the dad who is going to grow me up.'

Chrissy was very happy – she wanted Nico to feel secure and this was what he wanted. They had Jo and Jem's blessing.

'Thanks, Dad... Dad,' Nico said slowly, sliding off Thomas's lap, testing and loving the sound of the word.

Thomas smiled at Chrissy, satisfied that he would be good in his role as father to Nico in every sense of the word. Chrissy had brought his true sense of being into his life and she never stopped giving of herself.

The following day Chrissy had cried off work, as she was feeling very tired, and kissed Thomas farewell as she lay in the comfort of their bed. He had offered to stay with her, but she had persuaded him to go off to work as it was a very busy period with the merger and purchase of an adjoining building being finalised. Chrissy had inherited Kam as her personal secretary and Dina was flourishing as a caseworker in the criminal department. Barely had Thomas left the room than she had to make a run for the bathroom and was violently sick into the toilet bowl. She didn't trust herself to get up from the bathroom floor for the next ten minutes.

Chrissy went downstairs and felt cautious at the mention of bacon as AJ and Jo sat eating their breakfast. Chrissy poured herself some coffee and told the ladies about her sudden visit with the bathroom floor. AJ and Jo exchanged a conspiratorial look.

'What is it, guys?' Chrissy asked. AJ raised her eyebrows at Jo.

'Chrissy, have you considered that you might be pregnant?' said Jo, as AJ began gently bouncing on the spot in excitement.

Chrissy realised she had not had a period for three months, but she had never been regular, so hadn't really thought about it. Of course, she and Thomas wanted children but, oh, this was just perfect, she thought. Thomas would be so excited. Also, Nico would cherish being an older brother. Chrissy joined AJ, both of them jumping for joy. Jo stopped both their excited bouncing and chattering. 'Stop it, you two!' she said as she held both their arms.

'Chrissy, you have to try to eat something. AJ, see to that, will you, and Jem and I are going out to buy pregnancy tests.' With that, Jo ran off to find Jem, which she did, considering the pace at which he ran into the kitchen and hugged Chrissy, quickly returning to leave with Jo.

Chrissy telephoned Thomas, who was in a meeting and she left a message to ask him to call her back when he got out. He called an hour later, saying he was hungry for food – and her. She promised him a feast that evening and to hurry home. He asked if she was OK and she confirmed that she had never been better. Jem and Jo returned with the tests and the whole family traipsed up to Thomas and Chrissy's bathroom. Jo, Jem, AJ and Nico sat patiently on the bed, waiting for Chrissy to take the test. She emerged with the stick and they placed it on the bedside table. They then waited for the longest minute of their lives. To this motley group of people who were a family, there was nothing strange in this scenario. They were very much about sharing joy and sorrow.

Nico was a little confused about the whole procedure, but he knew that he was waiting to be told if he was going to get a baby sister or brother, and so was very excited. Chrissy and Jem first saw the word: 'Pregnant'. They jumped for joy. 'I'm pregnant!' shouted Chrissy, while, strangely, so did the others. There was a lot of hugging and kissing, and Nico made plans for the arrival of his new sister or brother.

Later that day Chrissy met Thomas at the main door when he arrived home and he kissed her slowly, easily swinging her into his arms and carrying her into the blue room. 'Oh,' Chrissy said, surprised, as he closed the door behind them. 'No, Tom,' Chrissy said, sure that the rest of the family were now outside the door.

'Come on, Chrissy, I haven't seen or touched you all day – I have really suffered,' he said, frowning.

'Poor baby,' Chrissy consoled him, as he rested his head against her chest and he began to caress her breasts through her top. Chrissy stayed his hands and held them in hers as she said, 'Just stop for a second, Tom.'

They both heard someone kick the door. Thomas looked at the door and got up to investigate. 'No, Tom,' Chrissy said too late; the whole family came spilling into the room as Thomas opened the door.

'What is this?' he asked them, confused, as they stood there smiling like idiots. Little Nico came forward and spilled the beans. 'Daddy, I'm going to be a big brother,' he said, acting like he had achieved this feat himself.

Thomas suddenly looked at Chrissy. 'Chrissy, Chrissy... is that right? Is you, are you...?' He stumbled for the first time in his life.

Chrissy nodded her head, smiling widely as Thomas whooped and lifted her clear off her feet, kissing her soundly as the family patted him on his back, and kisses were exchanged. Thomas picked Nico up and hugged him. 'Aren't we lucky, buddy?'

'Yes, Daddy,' Nico said proudly.

Two healthy identical twin girls were born to the family six months later. They had their mother's Mediterranean complexion, raven-black hair, and their father's blue eyes. Alexandra and Alicia. Their father and brother fell in love with them immediately. Two years later they were joined by little Leo, who shared Nico's black hair and black eyes. There was no mistaking they were brothers. All were adored by the whole family.

In the future, the three later additions would test the nerves of their older brother Nico through their numerous escapades.

Book Two

COMING SOON...

*N*ico would kill them if he ever found out about this, Alex and Ali thought, as they hid behind the bins of the seedy little dhaba in Ahmedabad. Both girls looked at poor Meera hiding with them. Meera was the cook at Amit's dhaba and Amit, the owner, had agreed that they could come to his dhaba and learn to cook from Meera. Obviously, Nico would blame them and their interfering natures, but it truly was not Alex and Ali's fault. They had to squat really low as the hiding space was so small. It was swelteringly hot today, the monsoon rains having briefly stopped to leave the city to bake for a while in the humid air. The bins stank to high heaven and there was mud underfoot as they shuffled to try to keep their footing.

Amit was hovering around and had passed them twice without noticing them. It had been a good five minutes since he last passed and so the girls slowly rose from behind the bins, anxiously looking around for him. It seemed clear, as they nodded to each other and made a quick sprint towards the taxi stand about a hundred yards away.

They ran for their lives as Amit spotted them and sprinted after them.

Book Two

COMING SOON.

ABOUT THE AUTHOR

Bhavna Chudasama is a criminal lawyer who has always had a love of reading romantic fiction. She was seventeen when she penned her first novel and has been published for the first time, aged fifty. In her view, everybody is deserving of love and romance in their lives and, even if they do not have it, they will find it in the story she has lovingly crafted for readers wherein the characters will always find their happy ever after.

Bhavna is of Indian origin and was born in Nairobi, Kenya. She has lived in east and south London and considers herself a south London girl. She is the eldest of six siblings and has a grown-up daughter. She describes herself as happily divorced and loves to be surrounded by her family and also loves her quiet time with her cats. If her writing career takes off, there will also be a dog!

Lightning Source UK Ltd.
Milton Keynes UK
UKHW040639210621
385890UK00001B/19